AT WAR IN NICARAGUA

AT
WAR IN
NICARAGUA

*The Reagan Doctrine
and the Politics of Nostalgia*

E. Bradford Burns

PERENNIAL LIBRARY

HARPER & ROW, PUBLISHERS, NEW YORK
Cambridge, Philadelphia, San Francisco, Washington
London, Mexico City, São Paulo, Singapore, Sydney

For
David John Aguayo

The following have been reprinted with the kind permission of the Center for International Policy, Washington, D.C.: "Multilateral Aid to Nicaragua" on page 31; "Structure of Nicaraguan Foreign Trade" on page 103; "Contadora. Key Aspects of the Treaty" on page 166; and "Contadora. The Treaty on Balance" on page 167.

The map of Nicaragua on page 55 has been reprinted with the kind permission of OXFAM.

FIRST EDITION

Designer: C. Linda Dingler
Copy editor: Rick Hermann

Library of Congress Cataloging-in-Publication Data
Burns, E. Bradford.
  At war in Nicaragua.

  Bibliography: p.
  1. United States—Foreign relations—Nicaragua.
2. Nicaragua—Foreign relations—United States. 3. United
States—Foreign relations—1981—   . 4. Nicaragua
—Politics and government—1979—   . 5. United States
—Military relations—Nicaragua. 6. Nicaragua—Military
relations—United States. I. Title.
E183.8.N5B48   1987   327.7307285   86-46124
ISBN 0-06-055074-0   87 88 89 90 91 MPC 10 9 8 7 6 5 4 3 2 1
ISBN 0-06-096188-0 (pbk.)   87 88 89 90 91 MPC 10 9 8 7 6 5 4 3 2 1

CONTENTS

ACKNOWLEDGMENTS

I owe special thanks to Richard Alan White and Donald Kalish for wise and helpful suggestions. I am grateful to the Office of International Studies and Overseas Programs of UCLA and the Institute on Global Conflict and Cooperation of the University of California for funding to carry out part of the research for this book. The students in my seminars on Nicaraguan history contributed significantly to this book. They fuel my faith in a just future.

ACKNOWLEDGMENT

INTRODUCTION

The United States is at war with Nicaragua, a war vital to ensure national security, according to President Ronald Reagan. In the struggle, the United States enlists only one ally, the Nicaraguan counterrevolutionaries known as the contras. The war isolates Washington from even its closest global allies, while it focuses international sympathy on Nicaragua. A country the mention of whose name once sent even the wisest to consult their gazetteers now enjoys almost daily front-page newspaper coverage from Washington to Wellington and hosts statesmen and visitors from every continent.

In the fixated vision of Washington and probably of Moscow as well, the curtain has risen on yet another act of the endless East-West drama. In the romantic vision of most of the world, the David and Goliath scenario plays itself out in the tropics. In the more intense vision of the Third World, an imperial superpower moves to crush the manifestation of independence by one of their small, underdeveloped peers. For the two-thirds of the global population composing the Third World, the war against Nicaragua challenges their hopes and aspirations. They see it as a highly visible symbol of an increasingly aggressive U.S. foreign policy. In the present struggle, they read the past and foresee the future.

For the United States, if certainly not for impoverished Nicaragua, the war is still small. Yet, the ramifications of this little-understood war will be far more serious than originally imagined because the repercussions for the United States are assuming global dimensions.

America enters this war as it did the Vietnam War in the early 1960s—with no concept of the immediate consequences or the longer-term repercussions of its actions. Only after four years of equivocating did the U.S. government clearly state the objective of the war: to drive the Sandinistas from power in Managua and to truncate the Nicaraguan revolution. Other questions will bedevil the confused American public. Why? How? What then? What costs? And what consequences? Mute, Washington provides no answers. Does it have any? More troubling than the silence is the lack of knowledge Washington demonstrates about the "enemy." Little wonder that the shadow of a Vietnam past casts itself ominously over a Central America present.

Unlike the U.S. intervention in Nicaragua in 1909 and the initiation of the U.S. occupation of that country in 1912, both of which caused barely an international ripple, the current war stirs waves that may yet assume tidal proportions. The world changed between 1909 and 1979. Colonialism, at least in its late nineteenth-century guise, died. A hundred wars were waged in the twentieth century to kill it. If there is any dominant theme in world history during the last half of the twentieth century, it is the dismantlement of empire. The more than one hundred nations of the Third World today testify to that theme. Catering to the politics of nostalgia in an increasingly sophisticated world bodes ill. Washington exposes its lack of a sense of realpolitik.

Ironically, the cry of the Nicaraguan revolution, "Patria Libre o Morir," is the direct translation into Spanish of the famous words of Patrick Henry spoken on the eve of the American revolution: "Give me liberty or give me death." His classic revolutionary speech of March 23, 1775, rings true two centuries later in the ears of many people in the Third World:

Are fleets and armies necessary to a work of love and reconciliation? They are sent over to bind and rivet upon us those chains which the British ministry has been for so long forging. . . . There is no retreat, but in submission and slavery. Is life so dear or peace so sweet, as to be purchased at the price of chains and slavery? . . . For me, give me liberty or give me death.

By a turn of the wheel of history, the oppressed during one era can become the oppressor during another or at least can be so perceived.

The fascination of the world with a war in Central America between the preeminent superpower and a plucky mini-nation arises from the knowledge that the conflict encapsules in microcosm the relations between the United States and the Third World. In the broadest possible interpretation, the war in Nicaragua heralds the possible emergence of a new international order in which the Third World can express itself without fear of repression from the superpowers. It is the axis upon which future relations between the superpower governments and their clients, between the developed and the underdeveloped nations, will turn.

In a small but significant way, Nicaragua offers an excellent opportunity for the United States to define a new policy toward the Third World and, if that policy be judicious, to exert a new leadership in the Third World and in the twenty-first century. However, if the Nicaraguan revolution is stereotypically cast in the by now rickety framework of the East-West struggle, then every hope for change anywhere will be classified as communist and attacked. If the United States will not tolerate revolution, change, development, and independence in Nicaragua, it probably will oppose those aspirations elsewhere in the vast and populous Third World. For those peoples, the stakes are very high in Nicaragua. For Washington, the stakes are higher than the leadership is willing to concede—or possibly knows. To crush Nicaragua will alienate the Third World, terminate any pretense of U.S. leadership in Latin America, and quite possibly diminish the U.S. leadership role among its European allies. Conceivably, it could detonate a political explosion that would shatter Latin America. At best, the victory, if there is one, will ring hollow.

Whatever happens now in Nicaragua, the relations of the United States with Latin America and, in a much broader sense, with the Third World will forever be different as a result. Having embarked upon this tumultuous sea of war, the American ship will need a skilled captain to avoid Scylla and Charybdis. This book attempts to point out some of the dangers of the present voyage and to indicate one chart to calmer waters.

I.
OBSESSED
WITH NICARAGUA

In Nicaragua, the United States is involved in the second longest war in its history. Only the conflict in Vietnam exceeded it—thus far.

The United States seeks to overthrow the government of Nicaragua, to replace it with one enjoying Washington's blessing. Obsessed with Nicaragua, President Ronald Reagan would like to use a surrogate force, Nicaraguan dissident exiles, to achieve that goal. The contras continue to prove themselves ineffective. Eventually Washington will have to commit U.S. military forces if President Reagan's goal is to be achieved. On June 25, 1986, by reversing two years of opposition and approving a $100 million budget for the contras, the House of Representatives took a significant step in that direction. Through that vote, the first "open" approval of funds to fight Nicaragua, Congress signaled its approval of President Reagan's policy. With memories of the event that intensified U.S. involvement in Vietnam twenty-two years earlier, some termed the action of Congress "the Gulf of Tonkin Resolution II." Whether it repeats history or not, it sets a historical precedent: For the first time, the U.S. government contributes money as an official policy to an armed group seeking to overthrow another government with which the United States maintains diplomatic relations and technically is at peace. The Central Intelligence Agency (CIA) will administer the funds and direct the war; the Green Berets will train the contras. As a logical consequence, war intensifies. Assistant Secretary of State Paul D. Wolfowitz reminds us, "It is from small wars that the greatest danger of big ones arises."[1] Hauntingly, the Vietnam analogy looms ever larger.

Nicaragua's Revolutionary Challenge

Nicaragua has witnessed many U.S. invasions and occupations. The dominant characteristic of its history, particularly in the twentieth century, has been the presence of the superpower lying to its north. To understand contemporary Nicaragua and its behavior, it is necessary to appreciate the fact that the Nicaraguans have enjoyed few years in this century in which they have been able to exercise even a semblance of sovereignty. Nicaraguans hoped to finally exert their sovereignty in mid-1979.

On July 19, 1979, after a long, costly, and bloody struggle, the people of Nicaragua overthrew the dictatorship of the Somoza dynasty. The father, Anastasio Somoza, Senior, and his two sons, Luis and Anastasio, Junior, had ruled Nicaragua since the mid-1930s. Somoza Senior owed his rise from lower-middle-class obscurity to political power and economic wealth to the United States. In the final years of the long intervention in and occupation of Nicaragua (1909–1933), U.S. military officials created a powerful National Guard to impose order and then appointed Somoza as its commander in chief. The position served as his springboard to the presidency and forty-three years of Somoza tyranny.

Most assessments indicate that venality and violence characterized the Somoza governments. While a tiny minority waxed wealthy and enjoyed every privilege during those decades, the nation remained underdeveloped. The overwhelming majority of its citizens lived in abject poverty, bearing most of the burdens of society.

A grim litany of statistics tells the tale. The population lacked health care, education, decent housing, and an adequate diet. Some of the statistics even reveal a further decline in the quality of life during the 1970s. In Nicaragua—as in Guatemala, El Salvador, and Honduras—the gap between the wealthy few and impoverished many yawned grotesquely. In 1975, the poorest 20 percent of the population had to make do with 4 percent of the national income, while the richest 20 percent enjoyed 55 percent.[2] Although unusually dismal, Nicaragua's human misery was not unique to Central America, nor the Third World.

A fundamental cause for the population's impoverishment was the unequal distribution of land. During successive coffee, banana, and cotton export booms, the large landowners expanded, pushing peasants off the land. The few monopolizing the land held most of it fallow or underused, mainly to ensure a ready labor pool of landless (and hungry) peasants.

In Nicaragua in 1963, although large farms of 750 acres or more constituted but 2 percent of the total farms, they enveloped 50 percent of the land. At the opposite end of the scale, peasants with 15 acres or less represented more than 50 percent of the total farms but only 3.5 percent of the land.[3] True to Latin American patterns, capital, technology, and labor concentrated in the rural export sector, the large estates. Scant resources remained for the smaller farmers and for the production of food crops, Consequently, food production failed to meet national needs. Nicaragua, like the rest of Latin America, imported food at prices only the small middle and upper classes could afford. The majority went hungry; disease preyed on the malnourished.

The Somoza dictatorship strengthened the institutions of the past that accounted for the poverty of the majority and the underdevelopment of the nation. Political repression accompanied, as it must, social and economic injustice.

Despite the high degree of rigidity the institutions exhibited, society itself changed. It became more complex. For one thing, rural folk migrated to the cities in increasing numbers. Between 1950 and 1975, Managua more than quadrupled in size to 432,000. One out of every five Nicaraguans lived in the capital. In that quarter of a century, Nicaragua moved from being a predominately rural to an urbanized nation. A modest industrial, banking, and commercial class emerged, often well integrated with the traditional landed aristocracy but still exhibiting distinct corporate interests and goals. Service and factory workers formed yet another significant new urban group. Students, intellectuals, and professionals more aggressively voiced their hopes and frustrations.

From that larger and more diversified society emerged the Sandinista Front for National Liberation (Frente Sandinista de Liberación Nacional, FSLN). Founded in 1961 largely by young intellectuals and students to challenge the static institutions and the dependency and poverty they fostered, the FSLN, as its name suggests, drew its inspiration from Augusto César Sandino, the guerrilla leader who had fought the U.S. occupation forces in Nicaragua (1927–1933) only to be assassinated by Somoza's National Guard in early 1934. His ideas guided the thoughts of the Sandinistas as they planned to regenerate the nation. Tomás Borge, one of the three founders of the FSLN and later Minister of the Interior, confirmed, "The thinking and ideas of Sandino are like an encyclopedia for the Sandinistas of today."[4] His Sandinista heirs raised him to the status of a national hero. Indeed, in death as in life, Sandino plays a significant role in twentieth-century Latin America.

To most Nicaraguans of succeeding generations, Sandino symbolizes independence, self-determination, nationalism, and social justice. The FSLN took his example as their guide; their "Historic Program" issued in 1969 reiterated his basic ideas. Also, Marxism—the young Nicaraguan intellectuals like their counterparts throughout Latin America discussed Marx and found relevance in much of what he wrote—and Liberation Theology—the substantive change of emphasis to social and economic thought within the Roman Catholic Church during the 1960s left a powerful impress on Nicaraguans—both mingle with Sandino's ideology as resurrected and elaborated by the FSLN. The FSLN led the armed struggle against the Somozas, a struggle that gained momentum after 1972.

The disastrous earthquake of 1972 did more than level much of Managua. It detonated an equally powerful political upheaval to topple the Somozas from power once the public learned the extent to which Anastasio Somoza, Junior, diverted earthquake relief funds into his own pockets and profited in every possible way from the national disaster. Disgusted by the endless corruption, larger and more varied elements of society joined the rebellion initiated by the FSLN.

An impressive coalition of political forces celebrated the revolutionary victory. Hatred of Somoza momentarily unified diverse segments of society. Following the course of all revolutionary histories, however, that coalition frayed when the difficult period of the "reconstruction" of society began. Opinions varied widely about the shape the new Nicaragua should take. Satisfied that Somoza was gone, some preferred that the institutions from the past remain intact. Others believed those institutions were too much a part of the past to continue unaltered into the future. The FSLN regarded the fall of Somoza as the prelude to fundamental structural changes, a profound revolution of society.

Drawing on its organization and determination honed by eighteen years of struggle against the Somoza tyranny, the FSLN labored to expand its popular appeal. By every indication, the party's leaders enjoyed wide support among the peasantry and workers—in short, the population base. The party's 1969 Historic Program provided a clear blueprint for the future.

An immense challenge awaited. The revolution inherited the earthquake-destroyed capital; the destruction left by a bitter civil war with its homeless, orphans, and wounded; an empty treasury; a foreign debt run up by Somoza in his frantic efforts to rearm the National Guard during the last years of the civil war; and all of the institutions of a dependent, underdeveloped past.

The problems overwhelmed the new government, and many still do after eight years. Replacing old, iniquitous institutions with new, hopefully more just ones has proven difficult. Mistakes have been made. While some complain that the revolution moves too slowly, others criticize it as precipitous. Hostility toward the revolution originates largely among the wealthy and middle classes, nervous about the loss of the privileges and powers they enjoyed in the past. At the same time, much of the intellectual support and the leadership of the revolution comes from members of those two classes. The humble classes, an overwhelming majority of the population, on balance defend the revolution. Indeed, that majority has benefited from it thus far.

Despite the hardships, war, poverty, and errors, the revolution has provided the majority of Nicaraguans with access to education, health care, and land—three primary desires of the once dispossessed. In 1980, a crash literacy campaign reduced illiteracy from approximately 50 to 10 percent. In 1983, more than a million Nicaraguans (40 percent of the population) were in school. The number of schools doubled between 1979 and 1984. Nicaraguans enjoy free education from kindergarten through graduate school.

Emphasis also falls on improved health care. It, too, is free. The government gives priority to rural health care, extending medical attention to the entire population for the first time. In the 1980s, hospitals have been built in most of the departmental capitals; clinics are ubiquitous. Nicaragua has practically eliminated measles, diphtheria, and polio, diseases that only a few years ago took a heavy toll among children. Doctors from all over the world, many from the United States, volunteer to treat patients. Meanwhile, Nicaragua works to train its own physicians. Prior to 1979, the freshman class of the medical school never enrolled more than fifty students; by the mid-1980s, the two medical schools accepted a combined entering class of nearly five hundred, a majority of whom were women.

A proper diet partially explains the improving health of the Nicaraguans. Caloric intake has risen because more basic foods are available to larger numbers of people. The Institute for Food and Development Policy of San Francisco reported that between 1979 and 1984 corn production rose 10 percent, bean production 45 percent, and rice production 50 percent. The consumption of those three staples climbed 33, 40, and 30 percent. In 1986, the Overseas Development Council observed, "Per capita consumption of nine out of eleven basic foodstuffs is reportedly still higher than before the revolution."[5] These achievements reflect in part the new investment priorities of the government favoring the countryside over the city. Capital investment in agriculture leaped 149 percent between 1978 and 1980; it increased by 34 percent in 1981 and by 126 percent in 1982. The statistics as well as the priorities contrast sharply with those of the rest of Central America. Between 1978 and 1982, capital investment in agriculture *dropped* by 57 percent in Gautemala and by 73 percent in Costa Rica.[6]

For the first time in generations, Nicaragua stands on the threshold of becoming self-sufficient in food. The achievement is highly unusual in Latin America, where nations import on the average about 25 percent of their food. (Venezuela imports more than 55 percent of the food its people eat.) Progress could have been even more spectacular had not the contras drained funds and labor from the fields of agriculture into the fields of combat.

Nonetheless, a far-reaching agrarian reform is moving ahead with increasing speed. It provides land for anyone who wants it and will work it. As the largest nation in Central America, Nicaragua has more than enough land to go around. The reform principally affects unused or underused land. Most of the land (the figure 60 percent is most often cited) remains in private hands. Putting the land into its most productive use to grow food for internal consumption and crops for export is the economic base upon which the revolution rests. A 1986 study by Professor Michael Carter, a University of Wisconsin agricultural economist specializing in agrarian structure and reform in developing countries, points out that Nicaragua's agrarian reform shows significant gains despite the heavy pressures of war.[7]

Fundamentally, the revolution that toppled the Somoza regime on July 19, 1979, arose out of underdevelopment. The national institutions had failed historically to benefit the majority upon whom society imposed increasingly heavy burdens and for whom it offered diminishing advantages. When a society senses and rejects that iniquity, circumstances are propitious for change. Indeed, new voices from a frustrated population demanded that change. Arising from those circumstances, the gathering strength of new social and economic realities shoved the Somozas from the Nicaraguan political stage. More importantly, the revolution effectively emancipated the poor, infusing in them a greater identification with and stake in the governing process.

Nationalism, Socialism, and Christianity converge to offer on a modest scale one model for the Third World. The model attracts international attention because it addresses the major concerns of most of the world's population. It challenges dependency, pursues economic development—the use of national resources for the greatest good of the largest number of inhabitants—embraces human dignity, and seeks social justice. After all, the access to land, the availability of health care, and the education that the revolution provides the Nicaraguan people are the very benefits that most of the people of the Third World crave.

The revolution will triumph through time if it continues to succeed in establishing its legitimacy as the embodiment of a more just society, a genuine expression of self-determination. To the degree the peoples of the Third World perceive the revolution's ability to embody both, it is widely received, even celebrated.

Nicaragua enacts in the final half of the twentieth century the drama of the Third World. Commandant Bayardo Arce captures this reality well when he asks,

Isn't the true threat of what is happening in Nicaragua and Central America that the small, poor, underdeveloped countries are offering a new term of reference to all of the Third World? How are the new social changes made that are needed by two-thirds of humanity so as to reach a minimum level of life and survival, while at the same time retrieving the dignity, respect, and self-determination that as independent nations our peoples are demanding now at the end of the twentieth century? These questions are not rhetorical. They attempt to raise a whole problematic: what we have called a challenge for the peoples of Europe, for the international community and its institutions, and very particularly for the North American people.[8]

In the eyes of the majority of the planet's population comprising the Third World, Nicaragua represents the dynamic of change.

In general terms, during the last half of the twentieth century, the United States, most of Europe and the Soviet Union, the white

Commonwealth nations, and Japan get richer; most of the rest of world remains poor. These poor nations want to improve their lot. They suspect the rich nations somehow prevent it. The current debt crisis confirms their suspicions. They manifest their aspirations for economic development through the Third World and Nonaligned Nations movements—and increasingly through the United Nations. Occasionally a bold, or desperate, Third World country challenges one of the dominant, wealthy, privileged nations, or is perceived to have done so, in an effort to increase its own ability to bring about change. In the 1980s, Nicaragua has done so. The Nicaraguans refuse to enter the twenty-first century shackled to the institutions of the nineteenth, a sentiment shared by all the people of the Third World.

The Traditional U.S. Response to Change

Throughout the twentieth century, the United States has greeted change among its client states in Latin America warily. Change has been equated with challenge, and challenges are not welcomed. Even reform governments—those that actually try to alter basic institutions, for example by nationalizing natural resources in the hands of foreigners, or by instituting a meaningful agrarian reform—often have felt the displeasure of the American government. The military overthrow of constitutionally elected and democratic President João Goulart of Brazil in 1964 and President Salvador Allende of Chile in 1973 not only bore the stamp of approval of Washington but enjoyed its encouragement and cooperation.

If Washington harbors serious suspicions about reforms, it abhors revolutions, those sudden, forceful, and often violent overturns of previously stable societies that substitute new institutions for those discredited. In fact, the U.S. government vigorously and physically opposed four of the five twentieth-century Latin America revolutions: Mexico (1910–1940), Guatemala (1944–1954), Cuba (1959 to the present), and Nicaragua (1979 to the present). It managed to co-opt, thwart, and then truncate the Bolivian revolution (1952–1964).

Similarities characterize the five revolutions (although notable differences also distinguish each from the others). All five had in common a desire to modify or eradicate traditional institutions considered incompatible with the drive for development. All recognized the importance of land reform in the restructuring of society and set about to radically change the landownership patterns. All were manifestations of intense nationalism. All involved the participation of ordinary citizens. All accelerated efforts to educate them. All favored one or another form of Socialism, greatly expanding the government's role in the economy. All hoped to increase their economic viability and independence of action. All favored greater industrialization. All removed from power—at least temporarily—representatives of the old oligarchy.

The fates of the five revolutions have varied. The Mexican revolution seemed to be succeeding until it grew rigid and conservative after 1940. The Guatemalan revolution was first halted and then reversed. The Bolivian revolution accomplished much in its first years, grew increasingly timid after 1956, and expired with the military coup d'état in 1964. The Cuban and Nicaraguan revolutions continue.

It took nearly three decades for Washington to reconcile itself to the new turn of events in Mexico, but not before it bombarded and occupied Mexico's principal port, Veracruz; blockaded the ports on the Gulf of Mexico; dispatched an army under General John J. ("Black Jack") Pershing to roam northern Mexico for a year; and applied every sort of diplomatic and economic pressure. Washington steadfastly opposed the Guatemalan and Cuban revolutions. In alliance with Guatemalan dissidents, the CIA succeeded in ending the Gautemalan experiment, and in cooperation with Cuban exiles, the CIA—perhaps with its Central American success in mind—later tried (at least once) to remove Castro and blunt the Cuban revolution. Thus far, its efforts have failed. The U.S. reaction to the Nicaraguan revolution has thus far been unequivocably negative. Only the Bolivian revolution received qualified support from the United States, and that aid went to the moderate wing that eventually came to dominate and reverse the revolutionary process. Such a consistent record of opposition to revolution doubtless reflects a nervous superpower fearful of change in or challenge from its client states.

Traditionally the United States has viewed the Latin American nations as its clients. The institutional structures of Latin America with roots burrowing into the colonial past complement and even accommodate that view. The trade, investment, and loan patterns established in the twentieth century favor the United States. Always sure of the geopolitical significance of Latin America, Washington is extremely cautious about hemispheric security questions, a sensitivity acutely evident since the treaty with Panama in 1903 to build the transisthmian canal.

The rise to dominance of the United States over the Western Hemisphere in the late nineteenth and early twentieth centuries coincided with the awakening and maturing of Latin American nationalism. The two trends set in motion an increasingly violent dialectic. Nationalism is a robust force seeking to terminate dependency and initiate development. The force stirs profound emotions.

Nationalism unsettles Washington, which has never shown much understanding of this most powerful force in contemporary Latin America. Denouncing "imperialism," i.e., the United States, the often fiery rhetoric blames the region's poverty on Yankee exploitation. In challenging the American government, the nationalists would weaken their ties to it. To further discomfort Washington, nationalism often embraces a socialist or neosocialist agenda. At any rate, nationalist rhetoric and revolutionary governments do not celebrate capitalism. In the minds of many North Americans, a lack of enthusiasm for capitalism can be interpreted as an inclination toward the Soviet Union. It sets off charges of "communism," often hurled at land reformers and advocates of greater social justice.

Washington concludes that change in Latin America threatens the dominant economic and diplomatic position and weakens the security of the United States. Consequently it has allied itself with those groups within Latin America least likely to advocate change: the traditional oligarchies and the military. Because those two groups are associated with the traditional institutions and by deduction with dependency and underdevelopment, they are under attack by the advocates and forces of change.

This international behavioral pattern plays itself out yet one more time in contemporary Nicaraguan–United States relations. The responses are Pavlovian. They testify to the wisdom of Thomas Hobbes's conclusion: "Prophesie being many times the principal Cause of the Event foretold." The action-reaction cycle is well under way in an escalation that has led to the first stages of war. The revolutionaries toss out the Somoza oligarchy and the National Guard. In turn, those two cry "communist takeover" to the cautious superpower already annoyed by nationalist rhetoric and apprehensive about agrarian reform, an independent foreign policy, and the nationalization of the banking system. Before too long, the oligarchy, National Guard, and Washington unite to oppose the "communists," i.e., the revolutionaries who advocate change. On this well-worn scenario, Senator Christopher Dodd, Democrat from Connecticut, comments, "Our present policy is folly because it identifies us with the status quo, if not the reactionary forces in the region, including former military commanders from the old Somoza National Guard."[9] Expressing the Latin American viewpoint, the Mexican intellectual Carlos Fuentes concludes that the old scenario itself will change, or at least its conclusion will:

A great power with a sphere of influence likes to feel that the smaller countries within its sphere will remain weak. Of course, with Nicaragua, Ronald Reagan claims: 'communism.' The problem, for Reagan, is the *independence* of the Latin American republics. There's a long history, a pattern, to what the Reagan administration is doing now in Central America. Now, with Nicaragua, the game has changed. The United States will not be able to do this anymore.

Perhaps the game has changed. Certainly it is in the process of changing. Whether the Reagan administration understands that Nicaragua can take greater command of its own destiny is doubtful. At any rate, seemingly oblivious of any game change, Washington follows the old traditional patterns of behavior.

U.S. Relations with Nicaragua

History and fantasy mingle mischievously in any discussion of the relations between the United States and Nicaragua. It is difficult to say which is the more fascinating—or fantastic. Often they contradict; often fantasy embellishes history. Generally, however, fantasy appears and reappears as the desire to ignore history, an effort to reshape reality. At no time has fantasy had more free play than at the present.

Nicaragua played a significant role in U.S. history during the mid–nineteenth century. With the acquisition of California in 1848 and the subsequent discovery of gold, people from the East flocked westward. Until the completion of the transcontinental railroad in 1869, the most popular route was by steamship to either Panama or Nicaragua, by mule, horse, carriage, or foot across the isthmus (until a railroad spanned Panama in 1855), and finally by steamship to San Francisco. Nicaragua offered an advantage to the travelers: only fourteen miles of land crossing.

Americans swarmed through that country, then in total disarray because of perennial civil war between the Liberals of León and the Conservatives of Granada, then the two principal cities of the underpopulated country. The Liberals contracted with the mercenary William Walker, a U.S. citizen, to fight their war. He joined up, only to defeat both political factions. After "electing" himself president in 1856, Walker served as the only U.S. citizen to be chief of state in Latin America. His rule was not an enlightened one. He reinstituted slavery—Walker courted the support of the Southern states in a North America deeply divided over the question of slavery. Since Walker did not speak Spanish, he decreed English as the national language. Generously he distributed Nicaraguan land to his North American followers. Nicaraguan history texts have nothing positive to say about the "Yankee president."

A war to expel the adventurer united all Central Americans. Defeated in 1857 by their combined armies, he fled—momentarily. Walker returned repeatedly to challenge and haunt the Central Americans until he died before a Honduran firing squad in 1860.

The experience alerted the Central Americans in general and the Nicaraguans in particular to the threat the North Americans posed to their enfeebled sovereignty. The Civil War and reunification, the construction of transcontinental railroads, the occupation of the West, and the industrialization process turned U.S. attention inward until the end of the nineteenth century. The quick victory over Spain in 1898, the consequent acquisition of the Philippines, Cuba, and Puerto Rico, and the determination to build a canal across Central America refocused that attention on the isthmus at the turn of the century. Nicaragua and Panama offered the most logical sites for the canal. Eventually President Theodore Roosevelt "took" Panama and initiated construction there.

Liberal President José Santos Zelaya, who since 1893 had been setting longevity records for holding the Nicaraguan presidency, reacted angrily to that U.S. preference. His hopes for the greater glory of his country included a prosperous international canal. He spoke vaguely of raising loans—perhaps in Germany, or in England, or maybe in Japan—to build a Nicaraguan canal. The United States, already deeply committed to and invested in the Panama Canal, rejected the idea, however vague, of any competing canal. Relations between the feisty Zelaya and a wary Washington deteriorated.

Washington judged Zelaya as a "tyrant," labeling him a menace to peace in Central America. On the other hand, Nicaraguan history books tend to regard him as a major nationalist president, a modernizer, and the national unifier—he reincorporated the Mosquito (Caribbean) Coast into Nicaragua in 1894. When two U.S. citizens were caught mining the Río San Juan, Nicaragua's major access to the Caribbean, in order to impede troop movements, Zelaya ordered them shot. That incident in 1909 provided the excuse for the United States to intervene to overthrow him. This historical lesson was unmistakable. The first Nicaraguan chief of state to attempt to act independently of Washington was overthrown by the American government. In 1909 began an intimate—if unhappy—relationship between the United States and its new Central American client state that set the tone for the twentieth century. The

United States linked its destiny with that of Nicaragua, more than with any other Latin American nation except Panama.

Unable to find a suitable Nicaraguan to sit in the presidential palace with the support of the Nicaraguan people, Washington repeatedly sent in the marines to prop up its candidates. Finally, in exasperation, the marines were stationed in Nicaragua, permanently from 1912 to 1933 with a one-year hiatus in 1925–26. Under Secretary of State Robert Olds summed up the political reality of the situation in 1927: "Until now Central America has always understood that governments which we recognize and support stay in power, while those which we do not recognize and support fall. Nicaragua has become a test case. It is difficult to see how we can afford to be defeated." Many Nicaraguans reacted with indignation to the occupation. Sandino initiated a guerrilla war against the occupying forces in 1927. After nearly six years of fighting him and with no victory in sight, the United States withdrew its last military forces in January of 1933. The diplomat and banker Lawrence Dennis suggested at the time why the marines found it impossible to defeat Sandino: "Moreover, these organized opponents of our intervention have the sympathies of the masses in Nicaragua and through Latin America, a fact which accounts for their abundant supplies of arms and their knowledge of the movements of the marines." Before departing, however, the marines established, trained, and equipped the National Guard to maintain order. As one last act, the United States appointed Anastasio Somoza as the commander of the Guard.

Most Nicaraguans regard the Somozas as a surrogate for the United States. Certainly the father and two sons maintained intimate relations with Washington. They unrestrictedly opened their country to foreign investments. Nicaraguan foreign policy faithfully echoed that of its mentor. Managua's votes in the United Nations and the Organization of American States duplicated Washington's. The CIA used Nicaragua to prepare its invasions of Guatemala in 1954 and Cuba in 1961. Nicaraguan soldiers participated with those of the United States in the occupation of the Dominican Republic in 1965. The United States could claim no more faithful ally in the Vietnam War than Nicaragua. Most Nicaraguans conclude that the Somoza years, the mid-1930s until 1979, signify the indirect occupation of their country by the United States. Mathematically, they conclude that the United States occupied their country directly from 1909 to 1933 and indirectly from 1933 to 1979, a total of seventy years of occupation. Further, today, they add that since 1979 Washington has supported the remnants of the National Guard, the contras, in a war against Nicaragua.

History gives every indication that the United States is obsessed with Nicaragua. For the last eighty years it has been involved intimately with that small, impoverished, and underpopulated Central American republic. Yet, whether because of ignorance, embarrassment, or arrogance, Washington seldom alludes to, never dwells upon, the past relations of the United States with Nicaragua. On the other hand, the Nicaraguans know well the history of their past dealings with the West's superpower. They cannot afford not to. Nicaraguans like to point out that being a neighbor of the omnipotent Yankee is much like having an elephant in one's living room. Even if the elephant does nothing, you cannot ignore its presence. More seriously, as Carlos Fuentes has observed, "Perhaps no other nation in this hemisphere—not Mexico, not Cuba—has been so consistently abused by the United States."[10]

Immediately following World War II, while the United States enjoyed overwhelming military and economic superiority in the world, Washington created special institutions to further strengthen U.S. dominance in the sphere of its immediate interest and influence. The Inter-American Treaty of Reciprocal Assistance (the Rio Treaty) of 1947, a defense treaty designed to exclude the infiltration of communism, and the reorganization in 1948 of the amorphous Pan American Union into the Organization of American States, a mechanism of hemispheric self-regulation, complemented Washington's aims both regionally and globally.

With close geographic proximity to both the strategic Panama Canal and the United States, Nicaragua became tightly enfolded into the U.S. security system. In 1945, the War Department indicated six areas within Latin America of special significance to the United

States either for strategic reasons or for their natural resources. One was "the Panama Canal and approaches within one thousand miles." That area clearly included Nicaragua. In reality, however, the Joint Chiefs of Staff redefined U.S. interests in 1946 to envelop the entire hemisphere, in effect a reaffirmation of the Monroe Doctrine: "The Western Hemisphere is a distinct military entity, the integrity of which is a fundamental postulate of our security in the event of another world war." Secretary of War Robert P. Patterson informed Secretary of State George C. Marshall in 1946, "We take alarm from the appearance on the continent [Latin America] of foreign ideologies." He had communism specifically in mind.[11]

Detailed policies to implement the system—itself a part of the wider Pax Americana—emerged in the following years. National Security Council Document 68 of April 14, 1950, listed the steps necessary "to support a firm policy intended to check and roll back the Kremlin's drive for world domination." The eleven steps included "substantial" increases in military expenditures and military assistance programs; covert economic, political, and psychological warfare "with a view to fomenting and supporting unrest and revolt in selected strategic satellite countries"; and the "reduction of federal expenditures for purposes other than defense and foreign assistance."[12] That 1950 document reads like a blueprint for the policies of the Reagan administration in the 1980s.

Government officials generously interpreted those documents, directives, and treaties during the heyday of the Pax Americana. The United States obviously had the power to enforce its own interpretations. Few seem to have been blunter in their interpretations than George Kennan, head of the planning staff in the Department of State in the early post–World War II period. He affirmed in 1948:

We have about 50% of the world's wealth, but only 6.3% of its population. ... In this situation, we cannot fail to be the object of envy and resentment. Our real task in the coming period is to devise a pattern of relationships which will permit us to maintain this position of disparity without positive detriment to our national security. To do so, we will have to dispense

with all sentimentality and day-dreaming; and our attention will have to
be concentrated everywhere on our immediate national objectives. We
need not deceive ourselves that we can afford today the luxury of altruism
and world-benefaction. ... We should cease to talk about vague—and for
the Far East—unreal objectives such as human rights, the raising of living
standards, and democratization. The day is not far off when we are going
to have to deal in straight power concepts. The less we are then hampered
by idealistic slogans, the better.[13]

While "idealistic slogans" were not abandoned, neither were
"straight power concepts."

Washington exhibited ingenuity in interpreting any treaty to fit
its goals. An excellent example occurred in 1961. Adolf Berle, an
old-line liberal and a top adviser to President John F. Kennedy,
opined that despite all the treaties to the contrary, the United States
had a right to intervene in Cuba. He defended the Bay of Pigs
operation in these terms: "The conventions protecting against intervention did not apply because the communists had intruded into
this hemisphere and, second, because Castro's government was an
openly constituted totalitarian government which is clearly outside
the provisions of the Treaty of Rio de Janeiro."[14] Such rationales
give Washington carte blanche to intervene—or do anything else—
within the hemisphere.

The evidence suggests that this mentality has pervaded all
post–World War II administrations. That mentality predisposes
Washington to suspect the worst of any proposed social, economic,
or political changes within the client states of the Western Hemi-
sphere. In official thinking, change, at best, opens a door to communist influences. Following that line of thought, Secretary of State
George P. Shultz can diagnose the contemporary crises in Central
America in these terms: "We consider the problem in Central
America basically to be Nicaragua, as supported by Cuba and the
Soviet Union."[15] He made no mention that millions of Central
Americans yearn for some change to reduce their dependence,
reverse their underdevelopment, correct some of the social injus-
tices, perhaps even to enhance national dignity. Shultz failed to

recognize that their frustrations with finding the avenues to change blocked might contribute to generating the crises.

During his initial two years in office, President Jimmy Carter attempted to infuse into Washington's Latin American policy a greater sensitivity. His administration signed the Panama Canal Treaty of 1977, attempted to normalize relations with Cuba, and pressured the dictatorships to curtail their human rights abuses. Unfortunately, events in Iran, El Salvador, and Nicaragua unnerved him as did the dispatch of Cuban troops to Ethiopia. His policies quickly returned to the traditional mold set by the East-West conflict. The intensifying civil war in Nicaragua demanded his attention. Responding to the emergency, he exhibited the same uneasiness about change in Latin America that traditionally permeates U.S. policymakers. Formulating policy proved difficult because events in Nicaragua consistently outpaced thinking in Washington. Also, Somoza himself proved to be uncontrollable. Furthermore, compared to the leaders of the Frente Sandinista de Liberación Nacional, the moderates were ineffective, a consequence of habitual, perhaps even inherent, disorganization. Questions persist about the extent of their popularity.

By periodically withholding military credits and economic aid, President Carter tried to pressure Somoza into improving his human rights record. At the same time, U.S. diplomacy minimized, even ignored, the role of the FSLN. Washington hoped to find some way to transfer power from Somoza to the moderates.

The United States lost considerable ability to influence events when a letter of August 1, 1978, from Carter to Somoza became public. The president congratulated the dictator on his improved human rights record. Both Somoza and his opponents interpreted the remarks as a U.S. endorsement for the dictatorship. Thereafter, Somoza refused any compromise; his opponents radicalized.

In the critical year and a half between January 1978 and July 1979, none of Washington's plans or initiatives succeeded. All classes and groups came to despise Somoza and the National Guard. Even the moderates regarded Washington's thinking as unrealistic in light of the rapid pace of events within Nicaragua.

After the FSLN captured the Nicaraguan government building while Congress was in session inside (August 23, 1978) and, in the following month, also captured five cities, ever larger numbers of Nicaraguans joined the ranks of the *muchachos* of the FSLN. In June 1979, the FSLN launched the final offensive, liberating every major city except Managua. As the civil war intensified, U.S. influence over events receded. Nonetheless, at the end of June, Washington proposed a plan for the Nicaraguans to move slowly from the resignation of Somoza through a series of mediated moderate governments to elections in 1981, keeping military power in the hands of the National Guard and giving Somoza's National Liberal party continued access to politics. It provided no role for the FSLN. Nicaraguans promptly labeled it "Somocismo without Somoza." Both the FSLN and Somoza rejected the plan.

In July 1979, as the National Guard rapidly disintegrated, the FSLN swept into power, triumphantly entering Managua on the 19th. The U.S. reaction equaled the occasion. Washington expressed a cautious cordiality and immediately made available $10–$15 million in emergency relief and added $8.5 million in September 1979 for economic relief.

Washington had second thoughts, particularly Congress. In August 1979, the Carter administration worked out a $75 million aid package, $5 million as a grant, the remainder in credits. Congress hesitated to approve it. The Senate required that 60 percent of the funds go exclusively to the private sector, the most conservative element in the revolutionary society. Not to be outdone on caution, the House attached sixteen conditions to the aid. These required, among other things, the exclusive purchase of U.S.-made goods, a prohibition on using the funds for any health or educational projects involving the Cubans, and spending 1 percent of the funds to publicize U.S. generosity. A failure to hold elections would cancel the aid. Congressional reservations about the revolution prompted an almost unprecedented secret session to further discuss the aid, delaying disbursement of the money until September 1980, fourteen months after the revolution occurred. Even then a final condition demanded the president's certification that Managua

was not "exporting revolution." The Nicaraguans wanted the aid, but in the package they also got the message from a suspicous Washington that the revolution was not really welcome. It chilled Managua.

Meanwhile, the revolutionary government was implementing the nonaligned foreign policy advocated in the Historic Program of the FSLN. Nonalignment unnerves Washington, which prefers its clients to be vocally anti-communist and pro–United States. Nor did Washington want Managua to be too cozy with other revolutions. President Carter hoped to distance the Nicaraguans from Cuba and from the explosive situation in El Salvador, on the threshold of its own revolution in late 1979. However, the Nicaraguans, recognizing conditions in El Salvador as similar to those that had necessitated change in their own country, sympathized openly with the aspirations of the Salvadoran rebels and apparently, prior to 1981, supplied them with a limited quantity of small arms. They also maintained close relations with Cuba. The FSLN appreciated that for years Havana had been a reliable friend in the struggle against Somoza. Cuba followed through after July 1979 by dispatching aid, technicians, and advisers, including military advisers. In truth, the new government applied worldwide for aid, all too cognizant of its dire need for immediate help.

Realizing the uneasiness of Washington, the Nicaraguans made efforts not to antagonize their powerful neighbor. They pledged to respect investments of U.S. citizens, which, by conservative estimate, did not exceed $100 million; and to honor the nation's international debt, much of which Somoza had incurred to arm his National Guard. Further, they checked the most radical elements, expelling the Trotskyist Simón Bolívar Brigade (a South American support group), suspending publication of the Maoist newspaper, *El Pueblo,* and publicly criticizing the local communists.

When Jimmy Carter left the presidency in 1981, U.S. relations with Nicaragua seemed to be more or less normal, if not overly friendly. Both nations were apprehensive about each other. Washington remained uncertain of the final political direction of its client; the client wondered how much change the Western

power would tolerate. Only later were documents to reveal
in 1980, President Carter had allocated approximately $1 mill.
for covert anti-Sandinista aid. His initiation of covert aid to cou.
terrevolutionary activity facilitated Ronald Reagan's subsequen.
military operations, making them more palatable to the Democrats.[16] Secretly the seeds of greater conflict had been sown.

Neither Ronald Reagan nor the Republican party sympathized
with the Nicaraguan revolution, nor, for that matter, did either
seem to understand it. No truth exists in the assertion that Sandinista excesses drove them to oppose it. The record indicates that
both unmistakably opposed it from 1979 onward. Sandinista efforts
at accommodation never altered their opinion.

In a radio address as early as March 1979, Reagan, running for
the Republican party's nomination for the presidency, declared,

The troubles in Nicaragua bear a Cuban label. . . . While there are people
in that troubled land who probably have justified grievances against the
Somoza regime, there is no question that most of the rebels are Cuban-
trained, Cuban-armed and dedicated to creating another Communist country in this hemisphere.[17]

Thus, four months before the advent of the revolution, Reagan set
the theme for his criticism of the Sandinistas: they constituted a
communist menace. He has struck doggedly to that belief over the
years. No mention was made or has been made of the complex
economic, social, and political causes of the revolution, nor any
effort expended to fit it into a historical framework. Not underdevelopment, not dependency, not persistent poverty, but communism subverted the Somozas' forty-three-year hold on government. Candidate Reagan publicly scolded Jimmy Carter for
withdrawing economic aid to Somoza: "This we are doing because,
according to the State Department, President Somoza is in violation
of our standards of human rights. He may be—I don't know."[18] The
1980 Republican platform echoed its candidate's views:

We deplore the Marxist Sandinista takeover of Nicaragua and the Marxist attempt to destabilize El Salvador, Guatemala, and Honduras. We do not support United States assistance to any Marxist government in this hemisphere, and we oppose the Carter Administration aid program for the government of Nicaragua. However, we will support the efforts of the Nicaraguan people to establish a free and independent government.[19]

That cryptic final sentence foretold future mischief. Throughout the campaign, Reagan and the Republicans blamed all the turmoil and tribulations of the Third World on the Soviets. They pledged to "roll back" alleged Soviet advances by increasing military aid and training to anti-communist guerrillas. Such firm policies, they predicted, would help the United States to recapture its position as unquestioned world power, either through a restoration of the Pax Americana or a campaign of global unilateralism.

Critics of Ronald Reagan have claimed that his goals in Nicaragua were unclear, even variable. The Los Angeles *Times* commented, "The Reagan Administration has no policy toward the Sandinista government of Nicaragua."[20] Such critics mistake means for ends.

Since his days as a candidate for the Republican nomination, Reagan has had a simple, unshakable policy: to overthrow the government of Nicaragua dominated by the FSLN, to terminate the revolution. Edgar Chamorro, a Nicaraguan who held high offices with the contras before leaving them in disappointment, reported that after Reagan's election but before his inauguration as president, his policy assistants promised that the new president would supply aid to the contras. Their professed goal was to defeat the Sandinistas.[21]

A variety of reasons constrained Reagan from candidly announcing his goal prior to February 21, 1985. For one thing, U.S. public opinion needed to be swayed to his view. The public has opposed overwhelmingly his adventures in Central America, failing to give Reagan as much as 33 percent approval in any major public opinion poll on his Central American policies. For another, for many years Congress, in particular the House of Representatives, remained recalcitrant. Legislation such as the Boland Amendment, in effect from December 1982 to December of 1983, prohibited the use of funds, "for the purpose of overthrowing the government of Nicaragua." The president had to consider not only the fact that the United States and Nicaragua maintained diplomatic relations with each other, but also the many international laws, treaties in operation, and even some inhibitions provided under U.S. law. International opinion also reduced the free play of U.S. power, even within the U.S. primary sphere of influence, Central America.

Consequently, the Reagan administration resorted to sundry euphemisms to explain its hostility to Managua, support of the contras, and refusal to negotiate with Nicaragua. From the beginning the president claimed that he backed the contras in order to interdict arms flowing from Nicaragua into El Salvador. However, the contras never captured weapons in that elusive or perhaps illusionary flow. Meanwhile the contras boasted to every journalist within earshot that their goal was to overthrow the Sandinistas. The White House employed other rationalizations: to force the Sandinistas to reinstitute political "pluralism," to make them negotiate seriously for peace in Central America, to extract concessions from them in the Contadora peace process, to require them to sit down and talk with the opposition leaders in exile—i.e., the contras—to annul the November 1984 elections and to hold new ones in which the contras could participate. The president often denied that he sought "to destabilize or overthrow the government of Nicaragua" or "to impose or compel any particular form of government there," as he phrased it in a letter to Senator Howard H. Baker, Jr., Republican from Tennessee, on April 4, 1984.[22]

Meanwhile, evidence exists that the Sandinistas tried, at least to some degree, to accommodate Washington. They claimed no arms shipments were made to Salvadoran rebels and promised that none would be. No convincing evidence exists that such shipments took place after Reagan assumed the presidency. They sent Conservative Arturo Cruz, a member of the ruling junta and a respected international banker, to Washington as ambassador, charging him with the task of restoring good relations; they were the only nation to sign the preliminary draft of the Contadora peace treaty; they offered to send home Cuban advisers; they pledged their willingness to sign a treaty with the United States in which Nicaragua promised that no Soviet, Cuban, or other foreign bases would be established on their soil if the U.S. ended its support of the contras; they agreed to every suggestion for open verification of treaties. Washington termed each offer a "propaganda ploy," refusing to discuss it. Washington showed no real interest in reaching any accommodation with the Sandinistas.

Once reelected to the presidency, Ronald Reagan felt less constrained to conceal his policy to "remove" the Sandinistas in order to replace them with a government acceptable to Washington. A few days after the reelection, addressing the tensions and terrorism abroad in the world, Secretary of State George Shultz warned the American public that the United States should not become "the Hamlet of nations." It must be prepared to "go beyond passive defense to consider means of active prevention. We must be willing to use military force. ... The public must understand before the fact that there is potential for loss of life of some of our fighting men and the loss of life of some innocent people."[23] Such statements from high administration officials constituted part of a campaign to prepare the U.S. public for more active global military involvement, including, of course, vital Central America. Furthermore, the administration wanted to associate the Sandinistas with terrorism. Among other charges, they stood accused of harboring terrorists and participating in international terrorism. In short, according to Washington, they were international outlaws whose removal would benefit world order and peace.

Reagan expressed increasing concern about international opinion of U.S. reliability as an ally. In his reiteration of the credibility and determination themes, his words echoed statements by President Lyndon Johnson in 1965, on the verge of major U.S. escalation in the Vietnam war:

Around the globe from Berlin to Thailand are people whose well being rests in part of the belief that they can count on us if they are attacked.

To leave Vietnam to its fate would shake the confidence of these people in the values of an American commitment and in the value of America's word. The result would be an increased unrest and instability, and even wider war.

In the minds of Washington officials, Nicaragua put America's resolve to a test, just as Vietnam had done during earlier administrations. A failure of the United States to reassert control over Managua somehow would become equated internationally with a loss of power. After all, if Washington could not dominate a little Central American republic, how could it expect to command compliance in the halls of global power?

In an unusually harsh statement in early February 1984, President Reagan bitterly castigated the Sandinistas and openly declared that the United States supported their "removal" unless they agreed to join with the contras to "form a truly democratic government."[24] Eschewing all past euphemisms on February 25, 1985, he stated that his goal was "to remove [the Nicaraguan government] in the sense of its present structure." When asked if that meant the overthrow of the Sandinista government, he replied, "Not if the present government would turn around and say 'uncle' to the rebels."[25] In short, the United States would not intervene if the Sandinistas surrendered to the contras. The following month administration officials let it be known that the only Contadora peace proposal it would agree to would be one in which the Sandinista government renounced its Marxist ideals, invalidated the elections of November 1984, and adopted a "pluralistic democracy" acceptable to the Reagan administration. The officials admitted the unlikelihood of the Sandinistas capitulating to such demands.[26] By early 1986, the Los Angeles *Times* concluded that Reagan sought a military rather than a negotiated settlement.[27]

In late February 1986, Reagan asked Republican congressional leaders to "lift the restrictions which now tie our hands." He requested money for the contras, the end of a congressional resolution barring the CIA from helping to overthrow the Nicaraguan government, and permission to use U.S. military personnel to train the contras.[28] To clarify presidential remarks, journalists questioned White House spokesman Larry Speakes if the purpose of U.S. policy was to overthrow the Sandinistas. Speakes replied, "Yes, to be absolutely frank."[29] Donald Regan, White House chief of staff, expressed himself with equal candor during his March TV appearance on *Meet the Press*: "We have to get rid of it [the government of Nicaragua] in some way or another. . . . What we want to do is to try to help those who are trying to overthrow that Communist government."[30] A Pentagon report indicated that the best way to help was through an invasion.[31]

The House assented to Reagan's policy. On June 25, 1986, by a vote of 221 to 209, it gave the president what he wanted: money for the contras, an end to restrictions on CIA activities, and permission to employ U.S. trainers for the contras. In this lengthy and lengthening war, this congressional vote marked the first open approval of military assistance to the contras. Given the World Court ruling on June 27, 1986, that U.S. support of the contras in their war against the Sandinista government broke international law, Congress now stands with the administration before the world community as a violator of international law. While the congressional vote is not the Tonkin Gulf resolution, it provides all the permission an "imperial president" needs to make war on the Sandinistas. Representative Julian C. Dixon, Democrat from California, concluded, "The president is leading our country down a dangerous course that may inevitably lead to increased regional conflict and military intervention."[32] The Los Angeles *Times* editorialized, "Members of Congress may try to deny the harsh truth of the matter, but they have finally given President Reagan carte blanche to wage his dirty little war in Nicaragua."[33] He was not slow to use it. Within days, he decided to give the CIA operational control over the U.S. aid. The reports circulating that the CIA plans to spend an additional $400 million in covert aid and training for the contras seemed to be confirmed by a Senate refusal to prohibit the CIA from using its contingency fund in Nicaragua. Somehow the $100 million became $500 million; appending $300 million in economic aid, the sum Congress was being asked to approve escalated to

$800 million. Senator Alan Cranston, Democrat from California, concluded, "The price tag will be closer to $1 billion than $100 million a year."[34] The president affirmed that he would never let U.S. "inaction" be responsible for a "Communist takeover" of Nicaragua.[35] The twenty-five thousand contras were to receive as much as the equivalent of one-third of the Nicaraguan national budget, which has to serve over three million people.

The news of congressional approval of Reagan's goal thundered across Nicaragua. President Danial Ortega called the vote "a declaration of war against Nicaragua."[36] Intervention in Nicaragua "would mean total war in Central America," according to him.[37] He warned, "This vote makes it clear that Nicaragua is fighting for its survival against direct intervention, which could lead to a Vietnam in Central America."[38] The Nicaraguan president was not the only one who saw a Vietnamese parallel. Senator Cranston, terming Reagan's plans a "hydra-headed monster," cautioned, "This could be a re-run of Vietnam. First American money, then American advisers, then American control of the wars, then American troops."[39] Voltaire's maxim seems particularly applicable to contemporary Nicaragua: "The animal is vicious; when attacked, it defends itself."

II.
THE DIRTY LITTLE WAR

The Economic Attack

A small, underpopulated, underdeveloped client state makes an easy target for a major world power. It can apply pressures with impunity. The client's economy feels the first pressure, probing its vulnerability.

In order to withstand economic aggression, the small state must succeed in finding alternative sources of imports and in establishing new markets for exports. In an underdeveloped nation, the question arises as to the extent to which economic aggression really affects the majority of the population. It more than likely hurts the upper and middle classes most since they earn the incomes necessary to buy expensive imported items and those incomes in turn depend heavily on an export economy. Against countries like Nicaragua, economic aggression would directly affect 20 to 30 percent of the population. The many news items, for example, pointing out shortages of toothpaste, toilet paper, and light bulbs in Nicaragua really indicated inconveniences for the privileged classes since most of the population traditionally went without those items anyway. The rest of the population feels the aggression more indirectly, but that impact can be further minimized if the nation grows most or all of its basic food crops. With the major exception of a basic item such as oil, if the nation does not produce it, such an underdeveloped economy may be less vulnerable to economic pressures than a complex, developed one. When the government is a popular one, more representative of the impoverished majority than of the privileged minority, perhaps that vulnerability is still lower since the sectors least afflicted by aggression control political power. Furthermore, rather than undermining the government, foreign economic aggression can strengthen the resolve of the population and its support of the besieged government. Still, all things considered, any economic pressure on a small nation from its powerful and wealthy neighbor bears down heavily.

Immediately after his inauguration in 1981, President Reagan began to squeeze the fragile, dependent economy of Nicaragua. As a first step, his administration terminated all financial aid and access to loans from the United States. In March, it blocked the remaining $15 million of the $75 million in foreign aid credits approved by the previous administration; in April, it canceled a $10 million credit line for the purchase of wheat; and in September, it suspended a $7 million AID loan. In 1983, the administration began to close the sources of conventional international loans from the International Monetary Fund, the World Bank, and the Inter-American Development Bank. As the major contributor to these international institutions, the United States wields commensurate power over their operations. They cannot ignore pressure from Washington, as the 1985 Nicaraguan request for a loan from the Inter-American Development Bank illustrated. In a blunt letter to its director, Secretary of State George P. Shultz warned that the bank risked loss of U.S. financial support if it approved an agricultural credit loan request of $58 million from Nicaragua. Since the United States contributes nearly half of the bank's capital, its director understood Mr. Shultz's message. Drawing nothing from the Inter-American Development Bank, the Nicaraguans again found the well of conventional multilateral loans dry. The graph on page 31 illustrates the dramatic drop of multilateral aid. The actions of the

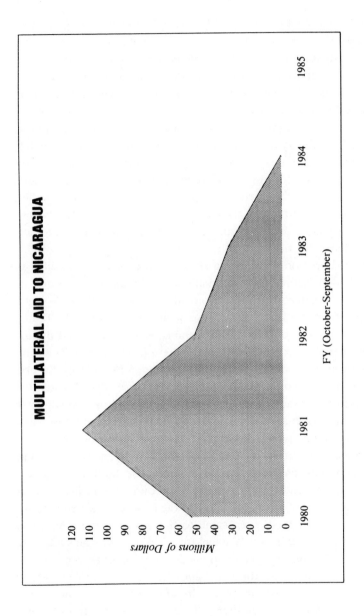

MULTILATERAL AID TO NICARAGUA

Millions of Dollars

FY (October–September)

multilateral banks had the additional effect of discouraging commercial banks from lending and foreign capitalists from investing.

If loans were one source of foreign revenue for Nicaragua, exports provided another. In May 1985, Reagan imposed a trade embargo under the provisions of the International Emergency Economic Powers Act. The president rationalized "that the policies
and actions of the Government of Nicaragua constitute an unusual
and extraordinary threat to the national security and foreign policy
of the United States." Washington closed the Nicaraguan consu-
lates, withdrew the airplane landing rights of Aeronica, and ended
trade between the United States and Nicaragua. It expected its allies
to participate in the embargo in order to increase its effectiveness.
Perhaps that is why President Reagan announced the embargo during a European trip.

World opinion reacted negatively. In the General Assembly of
the United Nations, the international community manifested its
"clear and categorical rejection of the economic blockade" by a
voter of ninety-one to six with forty-nine abstentions. The United
States counted Israel, Grenada, Gambia, Sierra Leone, and the nation of St. Christopher and Nevis as its sole supporters. The Latin
American Economic System (SELA), founded in 1975 by twenty-
five countries, condemned "economic measures that threaten the
sovereignty" of any member nation. The Caribbean community of
thirteen English-speaking nations (Caricom), unusually loyal supporters of U.S. policies, joined in the condemnation. In Central
America, both Costa Rica and Guatemala went on record in opposition to the embargo. Ignoring it in practice, both Honduras and
El Salvador continued trade and intercourse with Nicaragua. It
worked a kind of miracle within Nicaragua, where the fiercely anti-
Sandinista *La Prensa* even came to the government's support to
denounce the embargo: "We feel that President Reagan's response
is unjust."[1] The European nations and Canada criticized the U.S.
action. Response from the Nonaligned Nations and the Third World
decried the embargo. In effect, the embargo isolated the United
States, not Nicaragua. Minister of Trade Alejandro Martínez Cuenca
believed, "It hasn't hurt us politically. On the contrary, it helps us

because it is clearly evident that the aggressor is the United States."[2] In fact, here, as in other comparable instances, the "David and Goliath" image favored Nicaragua.

Nicaragua had prepared for the eventuality of such an embargo by diversifying its trade. As the hostility of Washington intensified after 1980, Nicaraguan–U.S. trade dwindled. Nicaragua sought out new markets and suppliers. For example, bananas that had once gone to the United States went to Western Europe along with new tropical exports such as avocados and mangoes. So did coffee, beef, and shellfish. The trade is not one-way. Nicaragua imports more from Europe, East and West, as well as from Canada, Japan, and Latin America. The Central American economist Xabier Gorostiaga noted, "We are not living in the '60s, when the blockade against Cuba began. Today you can obtain U.S. technology from Brazil, Mexico, Canada; the break will not be as severe as was the embargo on Cuba."[3] Minister of Trade Martínez Cuenca found that trade credits were easier to get from the Europeans than they had been from U.S. suppliers who preferred cash payments.[4]

The embargo has some unexpected effects. It probably hurts the private sector more than the public. It seems to spur some aspects of development by encouraging cottage industries to replicate replacement parts once imported. The government created a special "spare parts bank" and offers incentives to innovators who contribute parts to it. As early as 1981, through the Innovators Movement (Movimiento de Innovadores), the government encouraged workers to innovate and to invent in order to decrease dependency on foreign suppliers. In July 1985, Managua celebrated the First National Exposition of Innovators in Health Care featuring 106 exhibits of items produced locally but formerly imported. Officials estimated that the innovators saved the country millions of dollars in hard currencies.[5]

As of 1986, forty-three multinational corporations, including Texaco, IBM, Deere, Monsanto, Caterpillar, and Exxon, still operated in Nicaragua, accounting for approximately 25 percent of the nation's industrial production. They experience problems in repatriating profits. Otherwise, they conduct business pretty much as usual. Exxon refines Soviet oil now. Monsanto, no longer able to manufacture pesticides from raw materials from the United States, now imports them from the People's Republic of China. For diversification of trade and as an incentive to development, many Nicaraguans find a positive side to the U.S. embargo, but, putting the power of positive thinking aside, the embargo has handicapped the economy in many ways.

An early arms embargo constituted another U.S. pressure. Following the fall of Somoza, the new government desperately needed to equip an army. It applied to Washington, a generous patron of the Nicaraguan military since 1909. Washington responded with six thousand dollars' worth of binoculars and compasses! Nothing more was forthcoming. Managua then went to Western Europe in search of armaments. U.S. pressures on its NATO allies kept those doors closed. When Paris finally agreed to cooperate, selling $15 million in arms to Nicaragua in late 1981 and early 1982, Secretary of State Alexander Haig called the French action "a stab in the back." France delivered two coastal patrol boats, two Alouette helicopters, forty-five troop transports, one hundred missile launchers, and seven thousand missiles in 1982 and 1983. Under increasingly stronger U.S. pressures, France stopped supplying arms. In 1983, the Dutch spent $5.5 million to improve the harbor defenses at Corinto. Western Europe was not prepared to further defy U.S. demands for a halt.

As Washington blocked Western sources of armaments, the Nicaraguans turned to the Soviet Union for them. The action-reaction dialectic was in full play. Moscow responded positively. Ignoring both that Managua approached it first and that it refused the request, Washington charged that Managua's subsequent requests to Moscow were prima facie evidence of the triumph of communism in Nicaragua.

The Rhetoric of War

When war comes, warned Senator Hiram Johnson in 1919, truth is the first casualty. He might well have added that hyperbole takes on a new life.

As it became apparent that economic pressures would not topple the government in Managua, the Reagan administration intensified its rhetoric against the Sandinistas. The campaign had as part of its goal the winning of U.S. public opinion to favor greater support for the contras or whatever other steps were needed to make the Sandinistas "say uncle." Another part was to isolate Nicaragua, making it an international outcast. If the Sandinista government could convincingly be depicted as illegal, undemocratic, repressive, an exporter of terrorism, an international menace, a pawn of the Soviets or Cubans, or whatever, then a rationale would exist to overthrow it, to truncate the revolution.

President Reagan, who boasts a reputation as "the Great Communicator," seemed well qualified to present such a case against Nicaragua. In radio addresses, television appearances, press conferences, interviews, and several dramatic joint sessions of Congress, he forcefully expressed his opinions about that country and its government.

As his rhetoric rose in intensity in late 1984 and early 1985, he blasted the Nicaraguan government as a "brutal, cruel" regime without "a decent leg to stand on," "a Communist totalitarian state," "cruel totalitarians." The Sandinista leaders monopolized just about every evil imaginable and were contrasted—conveniently and inevitably—with the guys in the white hats, the contra leadership, our "brothers and freedom fighters," "the moral equal of our Founding Fathers," "lovers of freedom and democracy."

Oratorical excess drew a sharp rebuke from the press. The *New York Times* editorialized, "Instead of a reasoned case of a plausible policy, the Administration has chosen to mask war with whoppers, all the while condemning the Sandinistas as liars."[6]

Columnist Colman McCarthy complained, "A world leader is reducing himself to ceaseless diatribe. A pathetic spectacle is on display."[7] Trying to temper some of the presidential rhetoric, *Business Week* concluded,

But six years after its revolution, Nicaragua is still a partly open, partly pluralistic society, by contrast with the tightly controlled regimes of Cuba, the Soviet Union, and Eastern Europe. Opposition parties hold a third of the seats in a new National Constituent Assembly—more than in Mexico's Congress, for example. Despite the fighting, there are relatively few limits on travel in the country and abroad; Nicaragua's Catholic Church is strong and militant; and the opposition newspaper *La Prensa*, though censored, continues to print attacks on the government. There are even some Americans still running their own businesses in Nicaragua.[8]

Reagan would have none of it. If anything, he heightened the hyperbole.

The president's rhetoric did more than misinform the public. It misled Congress. In April 1985, Senators Tom Harkin, Democrat from Iowa, and John Kerry, Democrat from Massachusetts, released a study listing seventy-seven instances in which the administration had misled Congress on its policies in Central America.[9]

Some of the presidential charges against Nicaragua simply reflected historical oversight. The chief executive affirmed to *Time*, "The man whom they [the Sandinistas] honor, Sandino, he said he was a Communist,"[10] a statement that turns history on its head. Sandino repeatedly affirmed he was above all else a Nicaraguan nationalist; he turned away foreigners of every ideological stripe who came to proselytize; he expelled the Communist Agusto Farabundo Martí from his camp. Before his execution in El Salvador in 1932, Martí affirmed that Sandino "was unwilling to embrace the communist program that I stood for. He had raised only the flag of independence, of emancipation, while my aim was social revolt." No verifiable evidence exists that Sandino ever called himself a communist. History can only be revised if facts sustain the new thesis, although, properly controlled, imagination constitutes a historian's useful ally. However, imagination without facts is fiction.

Other charges depended at least in part on one's point of view. The president judges the Nicaraguan elections of November 4, 1984, in which the FSLN won 63 percent of the votes, a "sham." Among other things, he does not believe that the six opposition parties on the ballot enjoyed the same freedoms and financial support that the FSLN did. Others are less certain. European parliamentary delegations on hand to view those elections applauded them. So did Latin American and Canadian observers. A delegation of fifteen professors from the Latin American Studies Association, a U.S. organization of over three thousand U.S. academic specialists on Latin America, reported favorably on the November elections:

> The electoral process was marked by a high degree of "open-endedness," taking the form of continuous bargaining between the FSLN and the opposition groups over electoral rules and structures, as well as more general aspects of the political system and public policies. The record shows that both before and during the campaign, the Sandinistas made major concessions to opposition forces on nearly all points of contention.
>
> The national voter registration effort was remarkably successful, especially considering that it was conducted under wartime conditions. In just four days, 93.7 percent of the estimated voting-age population was registered.
>
> The Nicaraguan electoral law of 1984 provided a broad array of protections to assure fair access, procedural honesty, and an accurate vote count. The actual voting process was meticulously designed to minimize the potential for abuses. The vote was truly a secret ballot, and was generally perceived as such by voters. We observed no evidence of irregularities in the voting or vote-counting process.
>
> Despite efforts by U.S.-backed counterrevolutionary groups and several non-participating political groups to encourage voter abstention, 75 percent of registered voters cast ballots. Most voters interviewed by our delegation and by foreign journalists did not feel coerced into going to the polls.... The Sandinista government deliberately chose a West European–style proportional representation system that would maximize representation of opposition parties in the national legislature, rather than a U.S.-style single-member system.[11]

True, the FSLN is a powerful party. Its members, for one thing, work at grass-roots organization, an aspect missing historically from the activities of other political parties. Dominant, one-party politics are by no means uncommon in Latin America. Mexico has been virtually a one-party nation, the Institutional Revolutionary party, for the past half-century.

Other presidential charges misrepresent the facts. Such misrepresentations cannot be expected to produce successful policy. Reagan attacks the credibility of the revolution by oft claiming the Sandinistas had "literally made a contract to establish a true democracy" with the Organization of American States before taking power in 1979. Yet, as Roy Gutman in *Foreign Policy* points out, "According to the OAS, in a July 16, 1979, telex to then General Secretary Alejandro Orfila the Sandinistas said they planned to convoke 'the first free elections in this century' but made no reference to timing and said nothing about 'true democracy.' "[12]

President Reagan, Ambassador Jeane J. Kirkpatrick, and Assistant Secretary of State Thomas O. Enders, among others, often accuse the Sandinistas of exporting their revolution, quoting a description of the Nicaraguan revolution they attribute to them: a "revolution without frontiers." Thus, Washington concludes, the Nicaraguans menace other peace-loving countries. After Secretary of State Shultz employed the phrase, again attributing it to the Sandinistas, while testifying before the Senate Foreign Relations Committee in August 1984, Congressman Edward J. Markey, Democrat from Massachusetts, wrote him to ask for the source of the phrase. The State Department was unable to provide one. After continuing his search, Markey finally concluded, "Nobody could find a citation outside the Beltway [Washington]. We're positive it did not originate in Nicaragua." Markey believes the slogan was used "to lend credibility to the administration position that you can only deal by force with these people."[13]

Much more seriously, President Reagan depicts Managua as a haven for international terrorists. Conceivably this grave charge could serve as a pretext for bombing or even intervention. Contrary to presidential accusations, the PLO and Red Brigade have no representatives in Nicaragua. When contacted about this charge, neither the White House press office nor the State Department could provide any proof. The Italian government denies any knowledge of the presence of representatives of the Red Brigade in Nicaragua. At one time, Colombia did accuse Nicaragua as the source of some weapons captured from rebels in that country, but within a few days the Colombian foreign minister withdrew the charge.

No Nicaraguan fighters are known to be in Guatemala, El Salvador, Costa Rica, or Honduras as asserted, nor have any weapons from Nicaragua ever been captured in Guatemala or Costa Rica, as charged. Prior to 1981, Nicaragua apparently supplied a small quantity of arms to the rebels in El Salvador. At best, Washington presents circumstantial evidence of a continued supply, but it has never proven its case, and Managua denies it. The bulk of the evidence available confirms that the Salvadoran rebels get most or all of their weaponry from the regular Salvadoran army, either purchased or captured. Several years ago, the Nicaraguans apparently did aid a small band of Honduran rebels whom the Honduran army promptly obliterated. The Sandinistas understand their limitations. They realize it would be "suicide" to intervene in the affairs of their neighbors, and they do not have the resources for any "long-distance terrorism" even *if* they had the inclination.

Occasionally President Reagan brags of Latin American support for his Central American policies, using what the *New Yorker* refers to as "ghost facts."[14] The individual governments mentioned invariably protest, issuing a denial. On March 17, 1986, Reagan vaguely reported that a "Central American public opinion poll reveals that in some countries the rate goes as high as over 90% of the people who support what we're doing." No researcher has been able to locate that poll. Certainly it could not have been a Costa Rican poll, as inferred. A November 1985 poll in that country showed that only 39 percent of the Costa Ricans supported U.S. aid to the contras. In December 1985, the Costa Ricans elected a peace candidate, Oscar Arias, over a rival candidate who denounced the Sandinistas. Likewise, in elections at approximately the same time, the Guatemalans elected another peace candidate, Vinicio Cerezo. In fact, all of the Latin American governments support the Contadora Peace Process, even including Pinochet's Chile. Their support of that process places them in direct opposition to the Reagan policies.

Reagan indignantly accuses the Sandinista leadership of dealing internationally in drugs. The implication, besides constituting an affront to their morality, is that drug money sponsors Sandinista international terrorism. The *New Yorker*, along with other media sources, contradicts the president: "On drug-smuggling charges the President's own Drug Enforcement Administration has been on record all year long as saying that 'no evidence' has been 'developed to implicate . . . Nicaraguan officials' in drug trafficking."[15] The White House remains uncharacteristically silent about the contras' connection with drugs discussed in the press. In his monumental *Underground Empire: Where Crime and Governments Embrace*, James Mills considers Ronald Reagan's War on Drugs "a joke." His recent book cites Peru as the principal source of cocaine, Panama as "the world's cocaine banker," and Mexico and Colombia as countries whose drug profits "probably amount to 75 percent of their total export earnings." No accusations fall on the Sandinistas in the 1,165 pages of text.

The president frequently blames the Sandinistas for absence of any negotiations between the two governments. The Los Angeles *Times* bluntly corrected him:

At one point Reagan went beyond mere overstatement and simply did not tell the truth about U.S.-Nicaraguan relations: when he claimed that the United States tried to negotiate with the Sandinistas 10 times and was repudiated. Those bilateral meetings were not real negotiations because U.S. representatives went into them with a pre-determined position that they knew Nicaragua could not accept.[16]

Similarly, charges that the Sandinistas have destroyed free enterprise do not match the facts. About 60 percent of the economy remains in private hands, approximately the same as in France and far more than in Mexico or Brazil. Repeated statements that Nicaragua is a communist nation beg explanation. Three tiny, factious, communist parties exist: the Nicaraguan Socialist party, founded in 1944 and recognized by the USSR; the Nicaraguan Communist party, founded in 1971; and the Marxist-Leninist Popular Action Movement. They respectively received 1.3, 1.5, and 1 percent of the votes in the 1984 elections. Each occupies two seats, a total of six, of the ninety-six seats in the National Assembly.

The president wants to portray the Sandinistas as evil, the villains, the bad guys wearing black sombreros. In that aspect of his campaign, he has stated that they "summarily execute suspected dissidents." No proof of such actions exists. The State Department has had to contradict that charge. It has claimed that in 1984, the Nicaraguan security forces killed six political detainees. Yet, the Permanent Commission on Human Rights, a private Nicaraguan organization critical of the government, substantiates only one such case.[17] In a detailed 1986 report on Nicaragua's human rights record, Americas Watch concluded, "We are unable to detect in Nicaragua a deliberate, centrally directed practice of 'disappearing' detainees as took place in Argentina and Chile in the 1970s, in Guatemala from 1966 to the present and in El Salvador during the past six years."[18]

These examples represent a voluminous catalog of misinformation, disinformation, and questionable interpretations of fact, a catalog that led one wry commentator to refer unkindly to the Great Communicator as the "Great Fabricator." They prompted Roman Catholic Bishop Thomas Gumbleton of Detroit to shout from the steps of the Capitol on March 4, 1986, "In the name of God, stop the lies, stop the killing!"[19] Another Roman Catholic, Maryknoll Father Miguel D'Escoto, Foreign Minister of Nicaragua, also worries about the president's concept of reality. He, too, believes President Reagan has lied to the American public "with such mastery, with a great capacity for lying, for saying what is not so and for saying it with such serenity and such conviction, that I without becoming angry, felt an enormous sadness. And there came about a change in my vision of the problem that confronts us. . . . I thought, there is more in this than just a pathological obsession. . . . And one day, alone in my room, I thought that this incredible capacity for lying reveals something like a case of diabolical possession."[20] The president's words always make news. His charges repeatedly appear in print. Much of the American public believes them. The conclusion of the Austrian intellectual Karl Kraus rings true. Reflecting on the causes of World War I, he asked, "How is the world ruled and led to war? Diplomats lie to journalists and believe those lies when they see them in print."

On October 2, 1986, the Washington *Post* broke the story that the Reagan Administration had spread disinformation about Libya. The Department of State and the National Security Council concocted the plan approved by President Reagan and outlined in a memorandum written by national security adviser John M. Poindexter. It proposed a strategy that "combines real and illusionary events—through a disinformation program—with the basic goal of making Gadhafi think that there is a high degree of internal opposition to him within Libya, that his key trusted aides are disloyal, that the U.S. is about to move against him militarily." The major U.S. news media carried the disinformation about Libya as though it were the truth, unwisely confident that the news fed them by the government was legitimate. Later, after the Washington *Post* disclosure, the major newspapers huffed that they had been tricked, but the incident merely revealed the propensity of the press to print government handouts without asking questions. For its part, Washington reacted not by an apology to the press but instead by rationalizing the need to lie and launching an intensive search for the person who leaked the Poindexter memo to the press.

Anyone who closely follows events in Nicaragua eventually realizes that U.S. government statements about that country usually miss the mark. Since investigative journalism on Nicaragua is rare, the press seldom contradicts Reagan officials. The Poindexter memorandum on Libya has intensified suspicions that the government engages regularly in furnishing disinformation about Nicaragua in particular and about Central America in general. To assume otherwise would be to ascribe ignorance to high officials.

The presidential failure to distinguish fact from fantasy was nowhere so evident than in his speech of March 16, 1986, importuning Congress for aid to the contras. Anthony Lewis, in his op-ed essay "By Hate Possessed," concluded that Reagan's "obsession" with Nicaragua triggers his extremism: "When he spoke to the nation a week ago, urging military aid to the contras, his misstatements of fact were so flagrant that they troubled even those inured to Reagan fantasies."[21] Charging that misrepresentations and lies pervaded the TV address, a blistering editorial in the Los Angeles *Times* lamented, "No frontier snake-oil salesman ever put on a better presentation. Few presidents have put on a shabbier one. . . . [His statements are] all designed to screen the fact that the Reagan Administration is not satisfied with negotiating a peaceable solution but is determined to bring down the Nicaragua government."[22] Equally critical, the *L.A. Weekly* concluded, "No president in this century . . . ever delivered an address so riddled with fabrications, untruths, distortions, disinformation, and deceptions—all of it painting a picture of Nicaragua that exists only in Ronald Reagan's mind."[23]

These strong public criticisms of a specific policy stance echo broader conclusions of one former White House intimate, Budget Director David A. Stockman, who accused President Reagan of "self-deception." Looking back on his experience with the Reagan administration, Stockman concluded, "After four years [on the job], I had to conclude that what comes out of the White House type-writer is all hot air."[24]

Speeches such as the one of March 16 emphasize the president's belief that a complex world can actually be understood in terms of white and black, good and evil, anti-communist and communist, pro–United States and anti–United States. Thus, he divides the world and so compartmentalizes each event. It is the optic through which he views Central America. The Los Angeles *Times* editorialized, "It [the Reagan policy] manifests a regression to a simplistic anti-communism that is counterproductive because it fails to distinguish between real and imagined threats to national security. Perhaps worse, it risks deepening division among the nations truly important to the United States."[25]

The question of where the president gets his information is as intriguing as it is puzzling. Somewhere in the process of informing the president, a vast and expensive intelligence-gathering and -processing operation takes place. Embassies, the military, and the CIA, among others, collect information. To whom does this army of intelligence experts feed its data and what does it feed are questions concerned taxpayers and citizens should rightly ponder. One hopes the intelligence experts are better informed than the president. And yet, the record of the intelligence community is not all that encouraging. In 1961, for example, it promised that when the CIA-sponsored invaders reached the shores of the Bay of Pigs, the Cuban people in mass would rise up to greet their liberators and toss out Fidel Castro. Not one person arose. That tragic event passed into history as a monument to misinformation, wishful thinking, and a woeful lack of understanding of Latin American nationalism. One can ponder other intelligence disasters: the 1970 mission to rescue American pilots from Sontay prison in North Vietnam, the 1975 attempt to liberate the crew of the *Mayaguez* from their Cambodian captors, the aborted 1980 raid to free U.S. embassy hostages from Iranian revolutionaries, the experiences of the U.S. Marines in Lebanon between 1982 and 1984.

Recent leaks from the Defense Department whisper its conclusion that faulty intelligence marred the 1983 invasion of Grenada. The CIA did not know the location on the island of the U.S. medical students the invasion was supposed to rescue and evacuate. The intelligence data characterized the small Grenadian defense force the marines were to encounter as "poorly armed, low in morale" and with "only three or four [anti-aircraft] guns," each assessment incorrect. Grenada was an open society in the sense that any tourist with a camera could have photographed anything. Yet, a multibillion-dollar intelligence agency failed to gather correct information about an island less than twice the size of Washington, D.C. The Joint Chiefs of Staff, wise to the ways of the CIA, sent twice the number of men and equipment requested for the invasion.[26] The CIA symphonette plays a constant "They're low in morale" melody as part of the overture to intervention, whether it be Cuba, Grennada, or, currently, Nicaragua. After all, that is the music the White House pays to hear. Mark Twain considered military intelligence as a contradiction in terms.

In his thoughtful and thought-provoking book, *"The Target Is Destroyed": What Really Happened to Flight 007 and What America Knew About It* (1986), Seymour M. Hersh reminds us that intelligence is only as good as the use to which it is put. His exhaustive research proves that U.S. intelligence knew that Korean Air Lines Flight 007 had veered off course. Further, it knew that the Soviets had shot down the civilian airliner by mistake, thinking it was a spy plane. Although senior U.S. officials learned of the Soviet confusion in identifying KAL 007 as a U.S. reconnaissance plane, they nonetheless charged in public that the Soviets had identified it as a civilian jetliner. Hersh concludes, "The lesson from [the KAL 007] crisis is that none of the people had the intelligence they needed when they should have had it. And when they did have the intelligence, if it didn't agree with what they wanted, they ignored it." Every piece of public evidence available suggests that Hersh's insights and conclusions could apply to the Nicaraguan crisis.

As far as U.S. intelligence operations in Nicaragua are concerned, the public has been informed that our agents know at any given moment when "a toilet flushed in Managua." Perhaps, but the early November 1984 "MIG affair" raised some troubling questions about intelligence gathering and use—and manipulation. Washington informed the world that the Soviets were shipping MIGs to Nicaragua to challenge a stated U.S. determination that the Nicaraguans should have no sophisticated airplanes. The story dominated the front pages for days as the public followed the route of the Soviet freighter into the Nicaraguan port of Corinto with its crated cargo. By no coincidence, this blitz of news coverage occurred just as Nicaragua held its presidential elections. The newspapers devoted far more space to the MIG story than to those elections. The State Department, the Pentagon, and the White House each conveyed differing versions of what was happening, but when the crates were opened not a MIG was in sight, exactly as the Soviet ambassador to the United States had said would happen. Congressman Henry J. Hyde, Republican from Illinois, a loyal supporter of Reagan's Central American policy, complained that the MIG affair demonstrated a "lack of coordination and confusion which I view as a very disturbing situation."[27] Indeed, the question remains whether the intelligence community failed or whether the administration deliberately spread disinformation to divert the public's attention from the elections in Nicaragua. Either charge is serious. At any rate, as the Los Angeles *Times* notes, "The White House keeps producing reminders that the United States once followed a trail of misinformation and intrigue and tunnel vision deep into the jungles of Southeast Asia."[28]

While the historical analogy is not perfect, some general similarities chill the mind. In Vietnam, Washington offered first moral support, then some financial aid, and finally covert CIA support. When those three proved inadequate, American trainers arrived to teach the Vietnamese to fight. As of the vote in the House of Representatives on June 25, 1986, the United States has arrived at that point in Central America: The vote authorized U.S. trainers for the contras. The next step in U.S. involvement in Vietnam was to send troops.

Complaining loudly that Congress does not fund the war adequately, the administration never questions whether the strategy in Central America is correct. The June 1986 congressional vote signaled approval of the strategy, thus strengthening it, and rewarded Reagan's determination to funnel more money into the war in an effort to purchase victory. Reagan's position mirrors that of the varied administrations during the Vietnam War that insufficient funding, not incorrect strategy, hampered victory.

During the Vietnam conflict, a general vagueness of war aims prevailed. At times Washington spoke of the need to preserve—or establish, depending on who was talking—democracy in Vietnam. At other times, American involvement aimed to stop Chinese expansion or, taking another direction, to thwart Soviet aggression. Official explanations for U.S. involvement in the Nicaraguan war vary even more radically, as has been previously suggested. Vagueness in the pronouncement of public policy predominates again. One day the president announces that if the Nicaraguans do not accept "democracy" then the "only alternative" is for the "freedom fighters" to take over the government. On the following day, queried by reporters, a White House spokesperson insists that the remarks represent no change in administration policy.[29] Perhaps not, but it leaves the public mystified about which or what policy it is paying for. It should be a clear sign of swampy information and muddy thought.

More worrisome but as yet unexplored is the overlap of personnel from the Vietnam to the Nicaraguan wars. One dynamic duo immediately jumps into mind: Secretary of State Alexander Haig and Assistant Secretary for Inter-American Affairs Thomas O. Enders. Together they helped to plan and carry out the destruction of Cambodia from which, after more than a decade and a half, that small country still has not recovered. *Newsweek* reported that the two of them were a driving force behind contra operations, just the continuation of their cooperative efforts in Southeast Asia.[30] That duo breaks into a trio if we add Ambassador John Negroponte, a hawk in Vietnam, who became the proconsul of Honduras. To how many other men does Central America offer an opportunity to replay the Vietnamese drama closer to home where chances for success this time seem higher? The president, for example, believes that among other things indecisive leadership contributed to defeat in Asia, and he proposes to offer the steadfast leadership for success in Central America. Do these leaders see Central America as an "opportunity" to be seized rather than a problem to be resolved? In their minds, can military success in Central America dull the pain of military failure in Southeast Asia?

A lesson that Vietnam should have taught both the American government and people was that no war can be fought if the public is confused about the facts. Today the public is confused about issues in Central America; apparently so is the president.

In general, Reagan's policy in Central America is based on a misunderstanding of the region and the forces at play in it. Consequently fantasy masquerades as reality. Specifically the policy rests on a combination of untruths, half-truths, and truths, the latter constituting a minority. To be generous although malevolent, one might conclude that the president and his aids understand the fiction they propagate, but they do so in order to secure endorsement for their policy. To conclude otherwise is to expose ignorance in high places. However, in light of the administration's pursuit of a military solution to "the Nicaraguan problem," the president's statements do make sense: They constitute a rhetoric of war.

War is serious. So is national security. The president believes the security of the United States is at stake in Central America. For the embargo, he evoked far-reaching powers meant to be used only in the most serious and threatening emergencies. In April of 1983, he went on record signaling the gravity—at least to his thinking—of the situation in Central America:

The National Security of all the Americas is at stake in Central America. If we cannot defend ourselves there, we cannot expect to prevail elsewhere. Our credibility would collapse, our alliances would crumble and the safety or our homeland would be put in jeopardy.[31]

Echoing reams of rhetoric from the Vietnam years, this statement sums up the perception of reality of the most powerful man in the world. Not just the credibility of the United States, not just its alliances, but the very existence of the United States depends on overthrowing the Sandinistas and thereby reasserting domination over all of Central America. We may well challenge that perception of reality, but we must understand that it shapes the thinking within the Reagan administration. Those thoughts give birth to action. The rhetoric of war, too, must be taken seriously.

The Contra War

Historically when the American government disapproves of a Latin American government, it allies itself with the local elites and/or military to alter the political situation to its pleasure. Brazil in 1964, Chile in 1973, and El Salvador after 1979 provide three recent and classical examples of that behavior. In rare instances in which the military has been defeated and the elites denied ready access to power, Washington has no allies at or near the source of political power. Cuba in 1959 and Nicaragua in 1979 exemplify this unusual situation. In those cases, the United States through its own military and the CIA forges a force of exiles with the hope of using surrogates to regain its formerly dominant position. The surrogates, for their part, seek the spoils of power, the restoration of their own formerly dominant position.

In the case of Nicaragua, the President of the United States— working through the CIA—organized first members of Somoza's National Guard into a counterrevolutionary army and later amalgamated other dissidents and exiles into it. Then, after this was a *fait accompli*, the president approached the legislature for funding, having deprived Congress of any real role in debating the wisdom of the creation of a contra force or of declaring war in everything except name.

An "imperial president" such as Ronald Reagan shapes his own policy broadly, generously, by interpreting the law to suit it or, even more simply, by ignoring the law. He uses his power to bamboozle Congress into not only accepting but supporting it. Washington thus comes to terms with a new war in Nicaragua, while the American people have yet to come to terms with the last war in Vietnam. For that reason, even the "imperial president" encounters difficulties in commanding popular support for his policies. All major public opinion polls impressively reject the Reagan policies in Central America. Yet, the president pursues them and pressures Congress to march along with him, but both are out of step with the American people on these issues.

The United States maintains an increasingly strong military presence in Central America. The Department of Defense acknowledged assigning 12 military personnel to Nicaragua, 16 to Costa Rica, 18 to Guatemala, 119 to El Salvador, and 619 to Honduras in 1985. Except for Honduras, they serve mainly in the offices of the military attachés or as "trainers." On a much larger scale, the Pentagon stages extravagant and seemingly endless military exercises in Honduras and along the Caribbean and Atlantic coasts of Nicaragua. Those exercises began in 1981, when two were held; 1984 witnessed twenty such military exercises; from 1981 to 1985, the U.S. military engaged in forty such maneuvers. They vary in size. Ocean Venture '84, a two-week joint army, navy, air force, and

Marine Corps extravaganza employed 30,000 troops, an aircraft carrier, 35 ships, and 250 planes.

As a result of these almost continuous exercises, the United States has built an impressive military infrastructure in Honduras, trained large numbers of U.S. troops to fight in Central American terrain, and attempted to improve the quality of training of the Honduran army. The exercises are also meant to intimidate Nicaragua, although it is possible to argue that while they may inhibit the Nicaraguans they might also strengthen their resolve and intensify their sense of nationalism. The contras gain obvious advantage from them. They benefit from improvements in the military infrastructure within Honduras. Persistent rumors insist they also receive military equipment and other supplies through these exercises. They provide a protective cover for the contra activities. While none of these exercises trespasses on Nicaraguan territory, U.S. planes and ships regularly violate Nicaraguan sea and air space during their intelligence-gathering missions.

The CIA directs the major U.S. military project in Central America: the recruitment, training, and direction of the Nicaraguan contras. The president increased the agency's authority and mission in mid-1986. The headquarters for that extensive project is located in the U.S. embassy in Tegucigalpa, Honduras, where the ambassador serves as virtual proconsul. The stern, commanding, efficient John Negroponte fit that description perfectly during his tenure there. With the quantum leap in CIA participation authorized in Central America in mid-1986, the Reagan administration realized that Ambassador John A. Ferch, a career Foreign Service official, was not the right "field commander." Although on the job for less than a year, Washington summarily yanked him out of Tegucigalpa. A State Department official explained, "The Hondurans didn't like him, and the contras didn't like him."[32] Or, perhaps, the CIA did not like him. At any rate, a proconsul must enjoy the absolute confidence of the "imperial president." While career civil servants might be efficient, some doubt about their loyalty to a job rather than to a man might exist. An obviously angered ex-Ambassador to Honduras John Ferch complained later to the press that the

Reagan administration seeks a military solution to its dispute with Nicaragua. He termed the $100 million voted in June for the contras as simply a "down payment."

With some reservations and considerable uneasiness, the Honduran government and military cooperate with Washington, perhaps partly out of conviction but mainly out of hopes for financial benefits. Honduras is in a bizarre geopolitical position. Its real enemy is El Salvador, with which it fought a short but bitter war in 1969 and still conducts border disputes, but the Reagan administration demands that Honduras be friendly with El Salvador. Honduras has no bone to pick with Nicaragua, but Washington demands belligerence. A pitifully poor, underdeveloped, and dependent nation, Honduras sways with every breeze from the North. Roberto Suazo Tomé, the Honduran ambassador in charge of Mexican and Central American affairs, expressed that plight well: "We do not want to be more involved [in the Central American crises] but honestly we depend so much on the United States, it's hard to disagree with them."[33]

Honduras has been much more pliable than Nicaragua's neighbor on the southern flank, Costa Rica. Consequently, it has served as the major staging point for contra raids into Nicaragua. The strong U.S. and contra military presence in impoverished and enfeebled Honduras signifies to many local and international observers that jointly they occupy that nation. Whatever their desires might be, the Hondurans have no way to get rid of either occupying force, making Honduran sovereignty a fiction. Honduras will play a major role in any U.S. invasion or intervention in Nicaragua. For that reason, the Pentagon constructed and maintains an impressive infrastructure of ports, airfields, roads, camps, and radar stations throughout that nation.

U.S. determination to overthrow the Nicaraguan government rests, for the time being, on the contras. Following the fall of Somoza, nearly three thousand guardsmen fled to neighboring Honduras. Rumors of their intention to invade Nicaragua circulated even as jubilant crowds celebrated the advent of the revolution. Within a few weeks of the victory, Luis Carrión, a member of the

FSLN National Directorate, predicted, "We will have to face new kinds of aggression as a result of the organization of somocista forces outside the country."[34] In November 1979, sixty former guardsmen crossed the Honduran border into Nicaragua to initiate the war.

The CIA's hand was evident from the beginning. It had started collecting the scattered remnants of the defeated National Guard in July 1979 with the goal of waging a counterrevolutionary war against the new government in Managua, according to Christopher Dickey's account in his *With the Contras*. In her own book *Nicaragua: Revolution in the Family*, Shirley Christian pointed out that Colonel Enrique Bermudez, a career officer of the National Guard, organized the contra force in 1979 with several hundred thousand dollars from Luis Pallais, a cousin of Anastasio Somoza and once a leading figure in the Somoza government. Captain Armando López, a former member of the National Guard and later a contra, testified that officers and soldiers of the National Guard formed the original exile army, the 15th of September Legion, as well as the nucleus of the later Nicaraguan Democratic Force.[35] Dickey emphasizes that there would be no war in Nicaragua without the contras and no contra army without the United States. Washington recruits, organizes, trains, equips, finances, and directs them. Edgar Chamorro, a high contra civilian leader for four years, corroborates that conclusion.[36]

Although the Carter administration provided the original secret funding for the counterrevolutionary army, President Reagan has been much more generous in his support of it. Once in office, the Republican administration, through the office of Assistant Secretary of State Thomas O. Enders, immediately set about organizing and financing it. On March 19, 1981, the president authorized the CIA to spend $19 million for covert activities against Nicaragua. In November he authorized another $19.95 million to sustain five hundred contras.[37] The money came from the CIA's existing contingency funds.[38] For Colonel Bermudez and his band of warriors, those decisions answered their prayers.[39] Only in December 1981 did CIA Director William Casey report to the House and Senate Permanent Select Committees on Intelligence that Reagan had embarked on a secret war.

The CIA forged the National Guardsmen and increasing numbers of exiles disenchanted with the revolution and/or concerned with their loss of privileges in a new Nicaragua into the Nicaraguan Democratic Force (Fuerza Democrática Nicaragüense, FDN) in late 1981 and early 1982. In early 1982, the contras began to make serious attacks in Nicaragua. Efforts to dynamite two bridges in northern Nicaragua in March 1982 prompted the government to declare a state of national emergency. The war raged in earnest.

Contra morale soared and so did CIA expectations. A secret internal CIA planning memo of 1982 contained a timetable predicting the fall of Managua to the contra forces by Christmas of 1983.[40] By mid-1983, the contras bragged loudly of capturing the capital by December.[41]

The deepening U.S involvement in the intensifying conflict could no longer be kept secret from the American public. On November 8, 1982, *Newsweek* carried a special report, "America's Secret War—Target Nicaragua," revealing for the first time extensive details of U.S. participation in the war. In it, Washington announced its goal "to keep Managua off balance and apply pressure." *Newsweek* retorted that the real objective way to overthrow the Nicaraguan government. On April 4, 1983, *Time* exposed further details of the U.S. role in the war. By then the contras—often the CIA cloaked by a contra "cover"—were attacking fiercely and would continue to do so throughout the year, bombing the international airport at Managua, destroying 3.2 million gallons of gasoline and oil at Corinto, disrupting oil pipelines at Puerto Sandino, and attacking Pantasma. Captain Armando López boasted, "In 1983 we felt like one who had won the lottery. We lacked shoulders to carry all the weapons we got." Estimates of the size of the contra forces ranged erratically from ten to twenty thousand. The force definitely was expanding. Edgar Chamorro reported that the CIA exercised full control:

We [seven contra directors] first met with [Dewey] Maroni [the alias of Duane Clarridge, the CIA's operations director for the covert war] at one of our safe houses in Tegucigalpa in July, 1983. He was a powerfully built man with a barrel chest and a Bronx accent. He smoked cigars and spoke with authority. As he sat among us, he reminded me of a proconsul come to tell his subjects what do to and how to do it. I have never witnessed such arrogance while working with a foreigner.[42]

Chamorro concluded, "We were just the front. I felt we were manipulated, used as a figurehead."[43] The CIA called the tune because it paid the piper. It had supplied at least $80 million to the contra forces.[44] Further, the contras benefited from the food, weapons, and equipment left behind by the U.S. military exercises in Honduras.[45] In November 1983, a Congress growing nervous about U.S. involvement placed a cap of $24 million in aid to the contras for fiscal 1984. Despite the support and largess, the contras had to postpone any plans of Christmas in Managua. They did not even occupy a single village, much less the capital.

The Nicaraguan people spread no welcome mat for the contras, whom they associated with the hated Somoza past. In their judgment, the contras came not as liberators but to kill teachers, doctors, nurses, community leaders, and agrarian officials—the very ones who helped to ensure access to health care, education, and land, those popular achievements of the revolution. Even though many of the citizens were armed, no uprisings in support of the contras occurred. Chamorro recalls, "Our troops took the town of Ocotal once for a few hours, but the people didn't rejoice to see us."[46]

Audaciously the CIA stepped up the conflict, mining Nicaragua's major harbors, Corinto, Puerto Sandino, and El Bluff (see map on page 55). In classic Agent 007 style, commandos from a CIA "mother ship" slipped into the harbors aboard CIA speedboats protected by U.S.-piloted attack helicopters to lay the mines in January and February 1984.[47] The *Wall Street Journal* reported that between February 25 and March 28, five international ships hit mines, with serious damage to a Dutch dredger and a Cuban freighter;

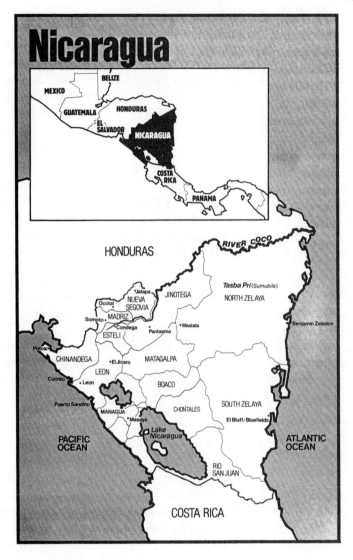

mines sank at least four small Nicaraguan patrol boats.[48] According to the Los Angeles *Times,* "Several Nicaraguan fishing boats, a Dutch dredger, even a Soviet oil tanker ran into them [the mines]. . . . The most serious loss: seven fishing boats."[49] *Barricada International*, a Nicaraguan newspaper, reported that the mines damaged nine ships from five different nations and killed eight Nicaraguan fishermen.[50] The mining outraged world opinion. Criticism cascaded over Washington. The U.S. press reacted negatively to the mining. Congressmen seethed with anger. The usually supportive Senator Barry Goldwater, Republican from Arizona, fired off a scathing letter of criticism to CIA Director Casey: "This is no way to run a railroad. I am pissed off."[51]

The mining caught no one more by surprise than the contra leadership. In the words of Edgar Chamorro:

At 2 A.M. on January 5, 1984, George woke me up at my safe house in Tegucigalpa and handed me a press release in excellent Spanish. I was surprised to read that we—the contras—were taking credit for having mined several Nicaraguan harbors. George told me to rush to our clandestine radio station and read this announcement before the Sandinistas broke the news. Of course, we played no role in the mining of the harbors. This was not unusual. The CIA often gave us credit (or perhaps blame) for operations that we knew nothing about.[52]

The October 1983 bombing of the Corinto petroleum tanks was one other example of CIA action in the contra name without the contras' knowledge.

This mode of operation duplicated the CIA's Cuban program in 1960–61, during the months leading up to the Bay of Pigs invasion. E. Howard Hunt, a CIA operative active in the preparations for that invasion, recalled in his *Give Us This Day* that the CIA really harbored contempt for the Cuban exiles and used them only when it suited its convenience: "Cuban [exile] plans, in any case, were not the ones that would be used on I-Day [the invasion], but plans that were being developed by the CIA and the Pentagon through the Joint Chiefs of Staff. Cuban military planning, therefore, was a harmless exercise and might prove tangentially useful if they became known to Castro's agents and served as deception material—disinformation. To paraphrase a homily: this was too important to be left to Cuban generals."[53] Indeed, the CIA locked away the Cuban exile leaders on the eve of the Bay of Pigs, and they did not learn of *their* invasion until after it occurred. A Madison Avenue public relations firm handled the news releases in their name.

The Bay of Pigs should have been a useful example from which the United States could learn. While history might not teach lessons, it can counsel caution. Certainly a quarter of a century later it offers at least some food for thought. One Cuban exile in the United States, Manuel Gómez, concludes that Washington misinterprets events in Nicaragua in the mid-1980s in much the same way it did in Cuba in the early 1960s:

The Cuban revolution was able to defeat the invaders, who were the contras of that day, for one very powerful reason: In the eyes of the majority of Cubans, the revolution had come to represent national pride and social justice. . . . Quite contrary to what my family and I wanted to believe, most Cubans didn't want the answer to come from the north, and certainly not through the barrel of a gun. . . . Some historians cite Castro's charismatic ability to fan the flames of nationalism as the chief reason for the counterrevolution's failure. But nationalism alone would not have been enough. The other critical component was most Cubans' fervid belief that the revolution had brought social justice. Again, for most of us who were against the government, social justice was a nice idea, but we didn't need it. We already had jobs, education, health care and so on. We agreed with the strategists up north that political freedoms were the important thing and, in typical fashion, we assumed that all Cubans felt the same way. . . . The Sandinistas, no matter what we think about them, carried the weight of defeating the Somoza dictatorship and raised the hopes of eliminating social injustice, and these are powerful weapons.[54]

Seemingly the CIA is reluctant to study the Bay of Pigs fiasco, even though some speculate the agency might be on the cusp of its repetition.

Meanwhile, other CIA operations were underway in Nicaragua. CIA helicopters made at least two raids, one on January 6, 1984, in the northern port city of Potosí, and another on March 7, 1984, in San Juan del Sur near the Costa Rican border. Americans, some with Vietnam War experience, flew those helicopters.[55] A secret CIA document listed nineteen similar operations in that time period. The number and intensity of the attacks apparently were greater than previously reported.[56]

As CIA involvement deepened, its problems increased. Obviously the burgeoning operations taxed its ingenuity to disguise them. The media did not always report favorably on what they uncovered or witnessed. Overly zealous agents attracted the wrong kind of attention. A major crisis erupted in October of 1984 when a manual prepared by the CIA in the name of the contras began to circulate. The ninety-page Spanish-language booklet, entitled *Psychological Operations in Guerrilla Warfare*, contained a highly controversial section, "Selective Use of Violence," that stated, "It is possible to neutralize carefully selected and planned targets, such as judges, police and state officials. It is absolutely necessary to gather together the population affected so that they will take part in the act." It further suggested hiring professional criminals to carry out "selective jobs" and advised arranging the death of a contra supporter to create a "martyr" for the cause.[57] In short, the CIA wrote and distributed a manual for terrorism at the same time President Reagan and high government officials were denouncing international terrorism in no uncertain terms and even taking armed action against it. The hypocrisy was obvious. The public outcry was unanimous. Again congressional ire was aroused.

In December of 1984, the House Select Committee on Intelligence charged the CIA with violating the congressional prohibition against efforts to overthrow the Nicaraguan government. The committee concluded, "The incident of the manual illustrates once again . . . that the CIA does not have adeqate command and control of the entire Nicaraguan covert action."[58] The committee was wrong: The CIA exercised total and absolute control over the contras. Ironically, it was Congress that exercised no control over the CIA.

Anger among the legislators prompted Congress in October

1984 to cut off funding to the contras from any agency "involved in intelligence activities." A resourceful executive found other ways to finance them. Lieutenant Colonel Oliver North, a White House liaison to the National Security Council, took charge of coordinating the contras, giving advice and helping them to raise more than $20 million in private funds.[59] The contras also received "money and equipment supplied by governments that are big recipients of U.S. aid—such as Honduras, El Salvador, and Israel."[60]

The congressional uproar did succeed in bringing some of the issues of contra funding from the shadows into the limelight. Thereafter, the president would have to ask openly for money, creating an unusual international situation in which the president of the United States requested funds to arm a people to fight a government with which the United States maintained diplomatic relations. The situation raised abundant moral and legal questions.

The multiple and multiplying crises prompted some realistic reassessments of affairs in Central America. "It is now clear that the contras will not march triumphantly into Managua anytime soon, if ever," concluded the Los Angeles *Times* and then added, "They [the contras] do not have the popular support needed to win a guerrilla war."[61] Senator Patrick Leahy, Democrat from Vermont, added, "You suddenly realize that we've got a multimillion-dollar covert action down there and every single objective is unattainable."[62]

In April 1985, the House of Representatives rejected the executive's request for funds to the contras by a vote of 303–123. Shortly thereafter, President Daniel Ortega, fulfilling a months-old obligation to visit Moscow in request for aid, flew to the Soviet Union for a state visit. Despite the fact that he also visited Western Europe, the trip annoyed Congress, and as a consequence the House, in June, approved $27 million in "humanitarian" aid to the contras. The turn-around vote tallied 248–184 for the measure. The administration interpreted "humanitarian" aid in the broadest possible sense to include even trucks and helicopters.[63]

The use—some would say the abuse—of the term "humanitarian" aid for supplying the contras sparked controversy. As defined in the Geneva Conventions and Protocol, humanitarian aid must be made available only on the basis of human need, not for any political purpose; offered impartially to all sides in conflict; go to civilians and noncombatants; and be provided through independent agencies that have not taken sides. Clearly this money for the contras fulfilled none of these basic tests for humanitarian aid. In fact, humanitarian aid to combatants is a contradiction in terms. It discredits the noble goals of true humanitarian aid. It violates international law and custom. Bishop Thomas J. Gumbleton of Detroit called it "nothing more than aid to an armed force—it has nothing to do with healing wounds, feeding the hungry or clothing the naked."[64] At the same time, late 1985 and early 1986, the CIA secretly infused at least $1.5 million into contra political activities.[65]

Adolfo Calero, a principal leader of the contras and the civilian chief of the FDN, recognized the "humanitarian" aid for what it really was. Grateful for the money, he predicted it would enable his men "to go beyond the stop-and-go performance we've had ever since we started . . . [and] to put on a serious, continuous effort against the Sandinistas." Anyway, Don Adolfo is a persistent optimist. Although he had missed his Christmas 1983 rendezvous with victory in Managua, he declared anew in August 1985, "We're going to the cities. We're going to the Pacific seaboard [where the country's population is concentrated] . . . . It will take a little time—a few months, I would say."[66]

Others issued less euphoric predictions. The Nicaraguan army was being better equipped. The troops had learned hard lessons in the lengthening war. They enjoyed public support. Morale among them was high. More peasants carried guns, and they, too, were learning how to combat the contras. A secret State Department document in mid-1985 confessed that the Reagan administration could not expect military victory from the contras.[67] Coming to a similar conclusion a few months later, General Paul F. Gorman, once commander of the U.S. Southern Command based in Panama, admitted than even with aid the contras could not be expected to win "in the foreseeable future."[68] They were correct. By the end of 1985, the Nicaraguans had driven the contras back into Honduras. After the expenditure of a minimum of $200 million since 1979, the contras had nothing to show for it. They still did not occupy an inch of Nicaraguan territory.

President Reagan remained undaunted. Oblivious to Latin America's threatening problems of poverty and debt, a Latin American economic decline unparalleled since the early 1930s, rising unemployment throughout Latin America, the dependency of at least ten nations on drug traffic to the United States for their economic well-being, and growing national and international protest of U.S. actions in Central America, he focused his attention and that of the nation on Nicaragua. Meanwhile, neighboring Mexico teetered on the brink of economic collapse. It seemed to matter not to the president that his dogged determination to support the contras drove Managua closer to Moscow, alienated all our allies, and weakened U.S. leadership. The war in Nicaragua represented his commitment to "roll back the Kremlin," and nowhere did that battle seem more important to him than in Central America. Hence, he concentrated America's energies on that single objective to the dismay not just of Latin American governments but of our European allies as well.

In 1986, Reagan boldly asked Congress for $100 million for the contras. The Senate agreed, but the House of Representatives refused the request in April. However, unable to resist the ceaseless importuning and relentless pressure from the White House, it capitulated on June 25, 1986. Fifty-one Democrats joined all but nine House Republicans in the 221–209 victory for the president's persistence. The vote lent a Democratic facade to Reagan's foreign policy obsession with Nicaragua. Undaunted by the World Court's decision on June 27 that aid to the contras violated international laws and treaties, the Senate on August 13, 1986, voted fifty-three to forty-seven in favor of the $100 million. The sum voted was substantial compared to the minimum of $200 million in public and private funding that had gone to the contras in the previous seven years. The ever-ebullient Calero enthused, "We can anticipate popular insurrection, massive defections from the Sandinistas, massive enrollment [in the contra army] and rebellions from the regional armies of the Sandinistas. There will be a more aggressive military strategy, because we want to show that the Sandinistas can be defeated."[69] The achievement of those goals was precisely what President Reagan wanted. If Calero was correct this time, then a light shined at the end of the tunnel.

The administration and its new Democratic allies chose to overlook the reality that no other nation in the world favored the contras; that after seven years, they still held no Nicaraguan territory; that they sparked no popular enthusiasm. "The reality is the contras do not have the people of Nicaragua with them," concluded Senator Paul Simon, Democrat from Illinois.[70] In the words of House Speaker "Tip" O'Neill, "This is the wrong policy, in the wrong place and at the wrong time."[71] Edgar Chamorro, who knows the contras far better than anyone in Washington, disapproved of any further support for them. He characterized the contras as the most "undemocratic force" in Central America, the combined product of the CIA, Somoza, and the Argentine military. (During the height of the military dictatorship in Buenos Aires, Argentine military officers helped to train the contras.)[72]

New aid promised to continue and intensify a war that wrought death and destruction for the Nicaraguans. From 1980 through June of 1986, war casualties on both sides claimed 31,290 Nicaraguans, a figure proportionately equal to 1.5 million in a country the size of the United States. The dead included 293 students, 103 teachers, 5 doctors, and 3 nurses, all civilian victims of the contras. As of February 1986, the war had displaced 120,324 persons. During 1985, the contras destroyed 55 health centers serving 250,000 people; 3 children's nutritional centers; 2 electrical plants serving 2,222 people; and 44 schools (damaging 502 others), leaving 60,240 primary school students and 30,120 adult education students without classrooms.[73] Some observers characterize the contra campaign as a war against youth. As of June 1985, victims of less than twenty-one years numbered 3,346 (189 of them under twelve years of age). The number of orphans was 7,852.[74] Economic losses vary in calculation from $2 to $4 billion. The war forces Nicaragua to raise its defense budget annually. Defense accounted for only 7 percent of the national budget in 1980; the percentage reached 45 in 1985.[75] Furthermore, young men and women who should be economically productive fight a war instead. The total impact is to delay development, not just in Nicaragua but throughout Central America. Every one of the five nations experiences the consequences of the war. Each has raised its military budget. Trade between the five Central American nations has slowed to a trickle, in particular hurting manufacturing since the total market of Central America is essential for efficient industrialization. Foreign investments decline. Investors are loath to put money into a region rocked by war. Capital outflow increases. For these reasons, un- and underemployment afflict the majority of the populations. The military option offers no solution to the long-term problems of the region. In fact, it exacerbates them. War in Nicaragua is a swamp in which the feeble economies of Central America sink.

The Contra Leadership

To overthrow the Sandinistas, the contras require a larger army, better weapons, stricter discipline, and more rigorous training. The generous U.S. aid voted by Congress in the summer of 1986 addresses these requirements. They also need a convincing unification of their squabbling factions, a popular program that speaks to the needs and desires of large numbers of people, the broad support of the Nicaraguan people, and military victories. Of these the contras have none, and part of the explanation lies in their own leadership.

The contra leadership comprises two separate but interrelated groups corresponding to their civilian and military wings. In early 1985, testifying before Congress, Langhorne Motley, former Assistant Secretary of State for Inter-American Affairs, affirmed that "the freedom fighters [the contras] are peasants, farmers, shopkeepers, and vendors. Their leaders are without exception men who opposed Somoza."[76] Reagan officials have assiduously painted this image since 1981. It is false. The *New York Times* has reported at length on the recruitment of the contra military leadership from the ranks of former members of Somoza's National Guard.[77] An April 1985 report of the Arms Control and Foreign Policy Caucus of the Democratic party stated that forty-six of the top forty-eight military command positions of the contras were being held by Somoza's former guardsmen. Christopher Dickey corroborates those figures in his book *With the Contras*. Two once-prominent contra leaders, Edgar Chamorro of the FDN and Edén Pastora of the Democratic Revolutionary Alliance (Alianza Revolucionaria Democrática, ARDE), have withdrawn from the struggle, complaining loudly that former Somoza officers dominate it. Another former FDN official, this one of secondary rank, Salvador Icaza, denounced the contras for the same reason. Rectifying some of its former statements, the Reagan administration issued a more accurate—although still vague—depiction of the contra leadership in 1986. It states that of the 153 most senior military leaders, 27 percent served in the National Guard, 53 percent were civilians, and 20 percent had been "comrades in arms of the Sandinistas."[78] James LeMoyne once pointed out in the *New York Times* that although the number of former National Guardsmen in the contra forces may be small in comparison to the total membership, "their influence proves to be great."[79]

The higher the officer in the contra command structure, the more likely he served Somoza in the National Guard. At the top of the contra military hierarchy stands Colonel Enrique Adolfo Bermudez, who entered the National Guard in 1952, serving all three of the Somozas over the course of more than a quarter of a century. In his last post under Anastasio Somoza, Jr., he was military attaché in Washington. There the CIA contacted him, and he has worked for them ever since. For many years, his chief confidant was Ricardo "Chino" Lau, "one of the most notorious and brutal National Guardsmen under Somoza. Even months after [Adolfo] Calero announced Lau had resigned from the FDN, Lau was still the last person to talk to Bermudez at night and the first person to talk to him in the morning."[80] Under Bermudez, the chiefs of logistics, intelligence, training, operations, and special forces, and the commanders of most of the largest combat units, are veterans of the National Guard. So are many of the company commanders.

Former National Guardsmen fighting for the contra cause are obvious links with the Somoza past. Much less obvious, particularly to U.S. eyes, are the civilians supporting the contra cause who profited from the Somoza dictatorship.

Since almost every Nicaraguan outside the National Guard turned against Somoza in the last year or final months of his tenacious and disastrous hold on the government, a kind of mini-Götterdämmerung he insisted on playing out in the tropics, the number of civilians who could not boast of joining the struggle against Somoza is minuscule.

The civilian contra leadership tends to be—or was prior to 1979—economically affluent, representative of a tiny elite or a small middle class. They prospered during the Somoza years, signifying that the institutional structures and perhaps the dictator himself favored them. Many supported the Somozas—or accepted them—and enjoyed the benefits of a society that rewarded them, a society in which they profited handsomely. Alfonso Robelo Callejas, once a Somoza vice-president, is an FDN director. Aristides Sánchez, another Somoza intimate, for years dominated the FDN along with his brother-in-law Adolfo Calero, and Colonel Bermudez. Privately the powerful threesome was referred to as "the Bermudez triangle."[81] Robert S. Leiken, certainly no friend of the Sandinistas, concluded that men once linked to Anastasio Somoza dominate the contra leadership.[82] Their new role imposes no unbearable economic hardship. Almost all the contra leaders are on the CIA payroll. Each of the seven members of the FDN directorate receives an annual salary of $84,000, tax free, compliments of Uncle Sam. At least until 1986, they handled the contra financing according to their own whim.

The revolution alienated those men because it challenged their privileges. It promised to broaden the political base to include the citizenry at large, to allow the once politically voiceless to speak. It pledged to open the doors of educational and economic opportunity to them. When the privileged understood that revolutionary rhetoric was becoming reality, they felt frightened, threatened in a topsy-turvy world in which their own welfare was being considered the equal of the formerly dispossessed. Many of them turned against a revolution which they accused of threatening their privileges. It is a natural stage of every revolution. The common goal — in the Nicaraguan case the overthrow of Somoza—had been achieved. Agreement on what would fill the political vacuum divided the population. The well-organized and determined Sandinistas put forth their Historic Program of revolution and found the popular strength to carry it out. Of the many who opposed that program, some went into exile in order to fight against it.

Among them were three very wealthy men who found favor with the CIA: Alfonso Robelo, Adolfo Calero, and Arturo Cruz, familiarly known as the Triple A. By the mid-1980s, they frequently appeared in photographs at the elbow of President Reagan. The three smiled amiably; healthy, handsome, prosperous-looking men with whom North Americans could readily identify. After all, they resembled Rotarians assembled for a convention. When they spoke, it was in impeccable English, so we could readily understand them as well.

Arturo Cruz, sixty-two years old, spent most of his adult life outside of Nicaragua. It has been estimated that from 1960 to 1985, he lived only one year in his country. Hence, he is less well known in Nicaragua than he is in Washington. He spent so much time abroad because he worked as an international civil servant and for the Inter-American Development Bank. Associated with the Conservative party, he supported the revolution in 1979. The revolutionary leadership, trying to take advantage of his international prestige and financial contacts, invited him to participate in the government. Later, the government dispatched him to the United States as ambassador, thinking that he, if anyone, could bridge the widening gap between Managua and Washington. He defected while serving as ambassador. Before the Nicaraguan elections of 1984, he and his son worked closely with Edén Pastora. He has been on the CIA payroll, but for how long is known only to him and the CIA.[83] Frequently he was talked about as a candidate for the presidency in the 1984 elections. After considerable maneuvering and hesitation, he declined to enter them, alleging they would be "insufficiently democratic." Nonetheless, he seems comfortable leading a war of sabotage and terror which has no democratic pretensions at all, and associating with an organization—the FDN—whose leadership has many ties to the dictatorship of the past. The *New Yorker* considers him "a certifiable democrat, and the one who has put the most emphasis on human rights."[84]

Alfonso Robelo, forty-six years old, is a very wealthy chemical engineer, now based in Costa Rica. He became rich as a cotton grower and cooking-oil processor in the years before the revolution. He organized a small social democratic party in the late 1970s and favored jettisoning Somoza. In 1979, he became a member of the revolutionary governing junta. In his enthusiasm, he announced that Nicaragua's future lay with socialism. However, the revolution soon proved to be too radical for his tastes, and he resigned from the junta. Like Cruz, he also has been on the CIA payroll.[85] He is too ambitious and opportunistic to enjoy the full trust of most of the contra leaders.

By far the most politically powerful of this triumvirate is Adolfo Calero, aged fifty-four. He managed Coca-Cola of Nicaragua. Serving as one of the leaders of the Conservative party, he played an active role in the opposition to Somoza. At one point, the dictator briefly jailed him during a businessmen's strike. While he would have liked to replace Somoza in power, he never advocated any meaningful institutional changes for Nicaragua. His critics maintain he wanted "Somocismo without Somoza" and suspect him as a longtime contact for the CIA. He is eager to leave Miami for Managua where he envisions himself as a future president.

Calero dominates the FDN, the strongest contra force. He enjoys enthusiastic support from the U.S. far Right. He has a proven ability as a fundraiser. Many question, however, whether he has any democratic convictions. Senator Tom Harkin, Democrat from Iowa, has known Don Adolfo for many years and believes he is primarily motivated by greed and a desire for power. Harkin says Calero "was not opposed to Somoza because of the dictator's political and human rights abuses. The reason he didn't like Somoza was because

Somoza had taken some of his money. He wanted to get rid of Somoza so he could get in there and take other people's money." Harkin classified Calero as "a Ferdinand Marcos before his time."[86] Apparently few quibble with the senator's rather brusque assessment.

Age stands out as a significant factor about this threesome. In a country in which 50 percent of the population is under eighteen years of age and in which the voting age is sixteen, these contra chiefs are considered to be "old men." That characteristic stands, also, if you compare them to the ages of the vast majority of the FSLN leadership, twenty to forty-five years old. (Minister of the Interior Tomás Borge is a notable exception.) The youth of Nicaragua simply do not know these men. And what they might know about them, for good or for bad, rightly or wrongly, associates them with the privileges of the Somoza past, the CIA, Washington, and contra terror. At best they might appeal to the over-thirty Nicaraguans, but that age group is probably not even a voting majority.

The intimate associations of the three civilian contra leaders within the business world of the Somoza era further dims their luster among Nicaraguans. A former banker, a former Coca-Cola executive, a former president of the Chamber of Nicaraguan Industries, these men were selected and are supported by the CIA for political leadership. They represent the past. They have not even bothered to frame a program for the future. There is no way they can convincingly claim to represent the Nicaraguan people. None of the three carries a charismatic image within Nicaragua. Popularity in Washington does not signify popularity at home. In truth, given the workings of Latin American nationalism, it probably awakens distrust and engenders disdain.

Only the most tenuous of alliances unite Calero, Robelo, and Cruz. They simply do not trust each other. In fact, such divisions permeate the entire exile community, a major headache for Washington. Exile politics resemble a turbulent sea of storms and countercurrents. Apparently the CIA spends much of its time trying to calm that sea. In order to weld the contras together as a somewhat unified opposition to the revolution, the CIA in 1981 organized

THE DIRTY LITTLE WAR

many of the exiles into a group that emerged in early 1982 as the FDN; it had to reorganize them again in August 1984 and, yet again, in February 1985. Still, the discord over who should control money and troops continued. In April 1986, the contra factions met with U.S. officials "to iron out their internal conflicts." Arturo Cruz stormed out of the meeting, threatening to resign unless the FDN was put under civilian control. Calero refused to put "his army" under anyone else's command.[87] Finally, for public display, the CIA forced the leaders into the United Nicaraguan Opposition (UNO), which theoretically increased the powers of Cruz and Robelo at the expense of Calero. But the UNO is an imposed veneer behind which the squabbling continues. Silvio Arguello, a contra and vice-president under Somoza, told the Miami *Herald*, "UNO was de-signed to do battle in [the U.S.] Congress, not to do battle on the frontiers with the people of Nicaragua."[88] Indeed, in the months after the launching of UNO, Calero, obviously reluctant to share his power, gives every indication of spurning Robelo and Cruz and continues to behave in the high-handed fashion that has charac-terized him since 1979.[89] Whatever the arrangements made for superficial agreement, the reality is that a larger, foreign force shapes the outward behavior of the Nicaraguan exiles: "They are being used as instruments of U.S. foreign policy by the CIA and the Reagan administration . . . and by the old Somozista gang to get back the money and power they lost in 1979," Edgar Chamorro insists.[90] The Cuban and Nicaraguan exiles share more in common than cohabiting in Miami.

Doubtless because of the many and divergent views separating the contras, they have never issued a detailed program of their social, economic, and political goals. Obviously they all oppose the revolution and the FSLN. They express strong sentiments in favor of the United States. They favor "democracy"; they believe in "cap-italism." They attack Cuba and the Soviet Union. They denounce "communism"; they harbor deep suspicions of "socialism." In prac-tice, while the contra leaders laud the blessings of free enterprise, they show little inclination, other than a passing rhetorical flourish, for political democracy.

These generalities beg the question of a specific program the contras would implement if they obtained power in Managua. Would they continue the agrarian reform program in place and functioning since 1980, or, like the counterrevolutionaries in Guatemala after 1954 and the military dictatorship in Chile after 1973, would they turn back the clock by seizing the newly acquired lands of the peasants and cooperatives and returning them to the former owners? Would their loan program continue to favor the small over the large farmer? Would health care continue to be free? How would they integrate the long-isolated Caribbean coast into the nation-state? What relations would they have with the Mosquito Indians? What plans do they have for development as opposed to short-term, cyclical economic growth? What would they do with members of the FSLN? Could the Sandinistas continue to publish *Barricada*? What organizational form would their government take? Would the banks continue to be nationalized? The list of unanswered, unaddressed, and unresolved policy questions is lengthy. The important point is that after seven years no one knows for sure what the contras would do once in power. Senator Richard G. Lugar, Republican from Indiana, asked the pertinent question: "I'd like to know what their program is...whether they believe in constitutional principles."[91]

The long silence, the failure to enunciate a detailed program, raise deep suspicions. They prompt many to assume that a contra victory would return Nicaragua to "Somocismo without Somoza." Edgar Chamorro says so frankly: "If the contras ever took power, they would simply replace the communists with their law-and-order regime and no one would be any better off....I am now convinced that the contra cause for which I gave up two years of my life offers Nicaragua nothing but a return to the past."[92] Many in the U.S. Congress share Chamorro's views.[93] Congressman Richard A. Gephardt, Democrat from Missouri, believes, "They [the contras] are not a credible democratic alternative to the Sandinistas."[94] Senator Daniel Evans, Republican from Washington, concurs: "I don't have a great deal of confidence that the current contra leadership, which the administration tends to support most avidly, is doing the job; and if they come into power, I don't think they would be a very good influence in Nicaragua."[95]

The conclusion is that no program has emerged because there is no consensus. Codifying a meaningful program would further splinter the factious contras. For the time being, U.S. financial support coupled with strong-armed CIA tactics hold the leadership together. That reality augurs poorly for their own future. It contributes to the conclusion that the contras will be unable to overthrow the Sandinistas or to find the internal support to hold power without overt U.S. intervention. The present situation eerily resembles that of 1909. If history can serve as any guide, a tragedy is about to be repeated.

Meanwhile, in the prelude, the grim atrocities mount. The contras contribute more than their share to them. Senator Patrick J. Leahy, Democrat from Vermont, pointed out: "There is a growing body of evidence that the contras have committed widespread violence against the civilian population. I am concerned that money from our government goes to an organization that commits atrocities. I have been given affidavits by victims of atrocities, terrible photographs."[96] The International Human Rights Law Group published a report at that time—alas, only one in a long series of such reports by international organizations—containing sworn statements from witnesses to murder, torture, and rape committed by the contras.[97] The chairmen of both the Americas Watch and Helsinki Watch visited Central America in an effort to reconcile reports of contra crimes with President Reagan's assurances that the "freedom fighters" did not commit such acts. They witnessed "a planned strategy of terrorism . . . being carried out by the contras" and concluded "the U.S. cannot avoid responsibility for these activities."[98] Reed Brady prints a bleak collection of testimonies in his *Contra Terror in Nicaragua: Report of a Fact-finding Mission, September 1984–January 1985*. He charges, "Since 1981, the contras have used American advice and dollars to terrorize the civilian population of Nicaragua."

The contras terrorize more than the Nicaraguans. Their activities spill over into three other Central American countries. A lawsuit

filed in Miami in May of 1986 charges thirty contras—including
Adolfo Calero—and American supporters with drug smuggling,
gunrunning, and acts of violence in Costa Rica. It ties several de-
fendants to a plot to assassinate the U.S. Ambassador to Costa Rica,
Lewis Tambs, and then blame the murder on the Sandinistas. Finally, it claims the contras participated in the plot to kill Edén
Pastora, the head of ARDE, a rival of the FDN.[99]

Ties between the contras and the death squads of El Salvador
have also been alleged. The former chief of El Salvador's intelligence service, Colonel Roberto Santivarez, identified Colonel Ricardo Lau—a former officer of the National Guard, former chief of
intelligence for the FDN, and confidant of Colonel Bermudez—as
an officer who "trained some of the country's 'death squads' and
helped organize the 1980 assassination of Archbishop Oscar Ar-
nulfo Romero." U.S. officials have confirmed that Lau did associate
with figures identified with Salvadoran death squads. They suspect
he participated in political murders. The captured diary of Roberto
D'Aubuisson, a former Salvadoran intelligence officer and candidate
of the far Right for the presidency, carried this entry for March 27,
1980, three days after the assassination of the archbishop: "Con-
tribution to Nicaraguans $40,000.00. Col Ricardo [sic] Lao . . . Con-
tribution Nica—$80,000.00."[100] The full extent of the connection
between the far Right in El Salvador and the Nicaraguan contras
has yet to be explored.

Honduras feels the major impact of the contras. Their presence
is tolerated out of pressure from Washington but greatly feared
nonetheless. The contra force may well be more powerful than the
inept Honduran army, and the Hondurans realize it. A parcel of
Honduras embracing 450 square miles of sensitive borderlands
now informally goes under the name of "New Nicaragua," an area
far larger than any of the independent nation-states of the Lesser
Antilles. The FDN populates and polices it. The former Honduran
population of twelve thousand fled long ago. Honduras has col-
lected no taxes in "New Nicaragua" for more than two years. At
best it holds only titular sovereignty. The contras engage in assassinations and brutalities with impunity within Honduras. A high-

ranking Honduran Foreign Ministry official confided, "We are concerned that some of the contras were involved in criminal acts."[101] Former Foreign Minister Edgardo Paz Barnica accused the contras of "horrendous crimes" and urged them to carry on their war in Nicaragua.[102] The newspaper *El Tiempo*, published in San Pedro Sula—the second city of Honduras and a major industrial, trading, and banking center—reported, "From the border zone of El Paraiso Department . . . came . . . protests from the inhabitants over the depredations of the contras."[103] Indeed, a delegation of Honduran farmers called at the U.S. embassy and the Honduran Congress in late 1985 to request the removal of the contras: "We have had it to the limit with these people. They are cold-blooded killers." They cited atrocities and abuses at the hands of "indisciplined, poorly trained, and violent" contra recruits.[104]

For Honduras, the presence of the contras and the U.S. military is bad for business. The coffee producers in the border region claim the contras and the war are responsible for serious production losses.[105] They create a climate of tension and uncertainty that frightens away investors and sparks capital flight. At a Rotary Club luncheon in Tegucigalpa in late 1984, retired Colonel Juan Ramon Molina, a former Minister of the Interior, told a roomful of businessmen that the war against Nicaragua "won't help our development." The interests of Honduras, the colonel continued, were neither represented nor protected by the United States, certainly not by the contras.[106]

Violence and corruption related to the presence of the contras escalated in 1986. In July, still-unidentified assailants fired grenades and automatic weapons into the house of a prominent contra leader in one of the most exclusive neighborhoods of Tegucigalpa. On August 4, a powerful bomb destroyed the car and damaged the home of radio commentator Rodrigo Wong Arevalo, a critic of the contras. Inexorably, the war moved from the border regions into the capital.

The funneling of hundreds of millions of dollars through Honduras to the contras—and the promise of more of the precious dollars—magnifies a greed long the hallmark of the Central American military. Much of the struggle among the top brass occurs discreetly behind closed doors. The public usually witnesses only the rise and fall of commanders. But in mid-August of 1986, with the promise of really big bucks on their way, the intra-military scuffling took place in public. An obviously divided officer corps physically struggled to grab the top positions in the army and easier access to the dollars. In the shameful scramble for the money, any devotion to country becomes the first victim, any duty to Honduras is subordinated to serve the superpower.

The dark clouds of greed and the distant thunder of public discontent predict a heavy political storm in the Honduran future. Bleak prospects suggest that Honduras rather than El Salvador or Nicaragua in the long run will be the primary victim of the Central American crises. *El Tiempo* editorialized, "We know what is the cause of the terrorism that is flowering more rapidly than we had expected: the presence of the contras with the complicity of the civilian and military authorities." It spoke of the people's discontent with the contras as a "powder keg" waiting to explode.[107] Washington authors yet another Central American tragedy.

Central America has remained relatively free of the drug production and traffic undermining the morality and authority of many South American and Caribbean governments, but suspicions continually surface that the contras engage in the nefarious business. Ironically the Reagan administration accuses the Sandinistas of drug smuggling while downplaying the evidence against the contras.

In a speech on June 7, 1986, Vice-President George Bush linked drugs and terrorism; he disclosed the existence of a secret presidential directive that pinpointed the drug traffic as a national security threat. Then he immediately charged the Sandinista government with trafficking in drugs to finance international terror.[108] No evidence exists to substantiate either charge. Bush did not mention the contras, despite the accumulating incriminating evidence of the involvement of some Nicaraguan exiles in the drug business.

U.S. law enforcement officials reported that contras in northern Costa Rica participate in drug smuggling. Their activities include refueling planes at clandestine airstrips and helping to transport cocaine to other Costa Rican destinations for transshipment to the United States. Individuals associated with both the FDN and ARDE participate. A secret CIA analysis alleged that two top ARDE commanders used cocaine profits to buy arms.[109] The San Francisco *Examiner* reported that "a major Bay Area cocaine ring helped to finance the contra rebels in Nicaragua."[110] The State Department acknowledged that some contras had taken part in drug sales but denied that any of the leaders were involved. Assistant Secretary of State Elliot Abrams admitted, "We have discussed this issue [drug trafficking] with the resistance leaders and have been assured in categorical terms that they will not tolerate the involvement of members of their organization in drug trafficking."[111] Known investigations do not implicate the leaders but they do finger lower-level contras.[112]

New evidence continues to accumulate. On June 23, 1986, the San Francisco *Examiner* published more information linking the contras and drugs. It pointed to one Norwin Meneses-Canterero as both the operator of a multi-million-dollar cocaine ring in the Bay Area and a contra organizer and financial supporter. Adolfo Calero admitted that Meneses-Conterero met at least half a dozen times with FDN leaders including Enrique Bermudez.

High-level contras are implicated in financial shenanigans. Irregularities have come to light over the accountability of the $24 million in "humanitarian" aid Congress voted for the contras in mid-1985. On February 24, 1986, the General Accounting Office reported that of the $12.2 million disbursed only $5.1 million could be accounted for. The remaining $7.1 million had been deposited in a Miami bank account to which only three men had access: Adolfo Calero, his brother Mario, and Aristides Sánchez. Adolfo Calero is the principal civilian leader of the contras. Mario Calero, who once worked for the Military Academy of Somoza's National Guard and maintained close ties to Somoza, serves as the paymaster for the contras; in April of 1986, he was under FBI investigation for possible arms export violations. Aristides Sánchez, the brother of the husband of Adolfo and Mario's sister, and once a wealthy landowner and close associate of Somoza, is a member of the directorate of the FDN.

What happens to the money after it is deposited remains murky. So does much of the contra supply business. No U.S. official seems able to assess the validity of receipts, to check out the many suppliers who did not appear in standard business directories, to establish the reasonableness of prices, to verify the actual delivery or receipt of items, or to account for where the $7.1 million went.[113] Congressman Leon E. Panetta, Democrat from California, puzzled, "But the problem is, based on the documents they have, we do not know where that money went, except that it went into a Miami bank account, and from there we do not know."[114] General Accounting Office (GAO) official Frank C. Conahan, testifying before a House subcommittee, confirmed, "There is no audit trail showing payments from the brokers' accounts [the two Caleros and Sánchez] to suppliers."[115] To which Senator Tom Harkin exclaimed, "Boy what a sweetheart deal this is. We fund the money, they send it to a bank in Miami, and no one has to account for it thereafter."[116] The senator added, "In sum, contra financial transactions are done 'all in the family'—the Calero family. This kind of arrangement smells of corruption. Americans don't tolerate such 'sweetheart deals' in our government. Surely we shouldn't when done in Nicaragua or Honduras with U.S. taxpayers' dollars. . . . The contras' financial apparatus, because of its ties to Calero and his family, should not inspire the trust of Congress or American taxpayers."[117] Later, taking a more thorough look at the accounts, the GAO confessed it had no proof of how $13 million of the allocated $27 million were spent.[118]

Time found that of $3.3 million entrusted to one contra only $150,000 actually got to Central America. Most of it went to companies and "individuals" within the United States, although $380,000 found its way to offshore bank accounts on Grand Cayman Island or in the Bahamas. A sizable chunk of money, $743,000, went to pay off the Honduran army; its commander in chief, General Walter López Reyes, received another $450,000.[119] Later, additional evidence indicated that at least $1.2 million of the "humanitarian" aid found its way into the bank accounts of Honduran military officers. Clearly the contras were bribing the Honduran military.[120] The final accounting for the funds has yet to be rendered.

Evidence of phony and padded invoices abounded.[121] The Miami *Herald* reported that in Costa Rica the contras "have billed the U.S. for thousands of dollars in food, clothing and other supplies that merchants say they never sold or delivered to the insurgents. Though their numbers never exceeded 385, the contras "apparently charged the U.S. for enough supplies to outfit 2,000 or 3,000 guerrilla fighters."[122] In Honduras, padded invoices help to enrich both the contras and the Honduran military.[123] Senator John F. Kerry, Democrat from Massachusetts, stated that he had ample evidence of contra leaders "diverting" private donations into "illegal activities." He mentioned drug smuggling and gunrunning. Senate aids confirmed that private donors complained to Kerry of the failure of high contra officials to deliver their donated goods.[124]

For their part, the contras deny the charges of corruption. One spokesman for them, Bosco Matamoros, suggested, "This is all a fiction with the purpose of strangling U.S. support for the resistance."[125] Secretary of State George Shultz agreed. In fact, he lambasted the GAO report on the issue of the misuse of funds as a "politically motivated attack to destroy the credibility of the contras."[126]

Other adminstration officials were less sure. Privately they acknowledged that contra leaders had "skimmed aid money" and had bribed Honduran army officers to support the contras.[127] In Miami, contra dissidents affirmed that contra leaders had defrauded the United States by submitting false receipts.[128] In fact, the CIA sacked three high-ranking contra officers for "misappropriation of contra funds": Captain Juan Alcibiades Espinal, Captain Ramon Morales, and Major Emilio Echaverry. All had been officers in the National Guard.[129] Congressman Michael Barnes, Democrat from Maryland, chair of the Western Hemisphere Affairs subcommittee, concluded, "It's fairly evident that the funds are not going where they were intended to go, nor where the State Department thought they went."[130] Congressman David Bonior, Democrat from Michigan, was harsher in his judgment: "The contra program has been rotten from the start."[131]

In his special plea of June 24, 1986, beseeching the House of Representatives to pass the $100 million aid package for the contras, President Reagan alluded to the accuracy of the charges of contra corruption:

> I share your concerns. Even though some of those charges are Sandinista propaganda, I believe such abuses have occurred in the past. And they are intolerable.
>
> As a condition of our aid, I will insist on civilian control over all military forces; that no human rights abuses be tolerated; that any financial corruption be rooted out; that American aid go only to those committed to democratic principles.[132]

That recognition of past abuses contradicted the president's earlier statements that corruption charges were "concoctions."[133]

Congressional concerns with, not to say suspicions of, contra corruption could be seen in amendments the Senate made to Reagan's $100 million request. Republican senators Nancy Landon Kassebaum (Kansas), William Cohen (Maine), and Warren Rudman (New Hampshire) insisted that no funds should go to any contras— groups or individuals—guilty of corruption, engaged in drug trafficking, or covering up human rights violations. The issue of contra corruption has been raised. It makes Washington uneasy. More eyes will focus on contra accountability than ever before. The attention could stimulate or strangle the contra cause.

The suspicion of corruption, the persistent tales of human rights violations, the reputation of military incompetence, the inherent political infighting, the failure to be politically attractive, and the long shadow of Somoza darkening the leadership are only some of the problems from which the counterrevolutionary cause suffers. Another is the Reagan hyperbole. No group of men could live up to his fanciful descriptions. These contras, whatever their merits, simply are not "freedom fighters," nor the "moral equivalent of our founding fathers." Such windy rhetoric invites ridicule. It allows

Congressman Gerry Studds, Democrat from Massachusetts, to quip, "Our Founding Fathers did not maintain bank accounts in the Cayman Islands."[134] Or Christopher Hitchens to retort, "The proper historical analogy for these people is not the Founding Fathers but Benedict Arnold."[135] Or Carlos Fuentes to chuckle, "President Reagan calls the contras 'freedom fighters.' That provokes fits of laughter in Latin America. A 'freedom fighter' is one who fights for the independence of his country against the dependence induced on it by the major regional power.... The contras are stooges of Washington."[136] Senator Harkin has been less kind to the contra "founding fathers." He calls them "murderers, torturers, and rapists."[137] Thought-provoking is the knowledge that the only government in the world supportive of the contras is in Washington.

III.

GLOBAL ISSUES

The View from the United States: Security

Washington believes it hears the not-too-distant rumble of "falling dominoes." The dominoes, of course, are the Central American nations. The fall symbolizes their submission to communist control. Following that line of thought, Cuba fell to communist control in 1959, Nicaragua in 1979. Thus, do not El Salvador, Honduras, and Guatemala totter, domino-nations in line ready to fall? Many in Washington believe so, particularly if the United States does not act vigorously to prevent their fall.

Preventing their fall inevitably has meant shoring up the present system, strengthening those very outdated and iniquitous social and economic institutions that create discontent among the dispossessed, impoverished majority. Despite the depressing social statistics of Latin America, it is difficult for Washington to appreciate the desire or need for change there because U.S. businessmen, bankers, and investors profit handsomely. From their viewpoint, the system works and works well. Washington reflects their contentment, sharing their view that a profitable system should not be changed. Arguments that an economically developed Latin America might be an even better trading partner meet skepticism at best.

To tamper with the system seems more than foolish; it denotes subversion of a variety more likely than not, so the argument goes, made in Moscow.

Historically it has always been the Russians whom the United States has feared most in this hemisphere. Russian expansion southward from Alaska prompted President James Monroe to promulgate his famous "hands-off" doctrine in 1823. A century later, fear of the "Bolsheviks" in this hemisphere gripped the U.S. government and subsequently shaped its behavior and policy in the region. Even though the Mexican revolution predated the Russian by nearly seven years, Washington linked the two by the 1920s. The other four Latin American revolutions, and most of the serious reform movements as well, fell prey to the same suspicions of communist influence. In the cases of Mexico, Guatemala, and Bolivia, no intimate relations with Moscow existed. Guatemala, for example, did not even have diplomatic relations with the Soviet Union. The presence of a few known communists in and near the government was sufficient to alarm Washington.

Cuba and Nicaragua picked up many lessons from the experiences of the earlier Latin American revolutions. They remembered how the CIA easily undermined and then toppled the government of President Jacobo Arbenz of Guatemala, while his army stood idly by. Nicaraguans also learned how a small elite and middle class allied with the CIA brought the reformist government of President Salvador Allende of Chile crashing down.

One lesson learned by the client states was that no one of them alone could successfully confront the power of the American government. They needed help; one kind of help could be obtained from another, more distant, and much less accessible, super-power—the Soviet Union. In some respects that lack of ready accessibility appealed to the Latin Americans. Distance mitigates power, signifying to them that the possibility of direct Soviet intervention, for whatever reason, is as remote as the Kremlin. Distance might make the second superpower more acceptable.

Needless to say, Washington does not share those thoughts. Officials believe that Soviet intervention, or at least some sort of pres-

ence, is all too possible and permanent. They envision the establishment of Soviet military bases for war planes, spy planes,
submarines, or possibly even missiles. Indeed, a small number of
Soviet soldiers are stationed in Cuba. By no stretch of the imagination do their small numbers constitute a threat to the United
States. Still, the precedent discomforts Washington, which will not
tolerate its repetition.

The Somoza government recognized the Soviet Union in 1944,
but the two countries did not exchange diplomats until 1980. Moscow had not backed the revolution in 1979. As always, it lumbered
far behind reality, by now a tradition of both local communist
parties and the USSR, to which both Cuba and El Salvador bear
witness. Beginning in March of 1980, Managua and Moscow signed
accords for trade, aid, and cultural exchange. Military supplies
would follow later. The record is clear: As Washington's relations
with Nicaragua chilled, Moscow's warmed. In a special report for
the Department of State, Dr. C. G. Jacobsen of the University of
Miami concluded,

Moscow's presence in Central America emerges as both more extensive
and more multifaceted than generally appreciated. Her military and economic involvement is complemented by a slew of other contact points,
political, cultural, and professional. Yet Moscow's ability to control events
may ironically be less than commensurate. The counterweights to Soviet
influence are also more far-reaching and varied than sometimes appreciated. . . .

Moscow conceded that Washington's "right" to intervene in Nicaragua
was analagous to hers in Afghanistan. And she clearly half-expected that
the US *would* intervene ever-more forcefully. She openly stated that, in
the event of a full-scale American invasion, the Soviet response would be
restricted to "solidarity," and "full political support." She had striven to
give Managua the means, but the bottom line was that the Sandinistas
would indeed have to defend themselves. Finally, one must note that Moscow apparently expects to benefit whatever the course of events. She
appears to calculate that the political-ideological PR harvest that would
accrue from an all-out US invasion would outweigh the loss of immediate
advantage.[1]

The Jacobsen Report emphasizes Moscow's caution. While it offers "political support," it has never pledged it would protect Nicaragua militarily.

Washington remains sensitive to any Soviet presence. Even cordial relations between a Latin American nation and the USSR raise serious security concerns of possible Soviet influence. In the post–World War II decade, few Latin American nations maintained diplomatic relations with the Soviet Union; in the 1980s, almost all of them do. As late as the 1960s, Moscow had diplomatic relations in South America with only Argentina, Uruguay, and Brazil; in the 1980s, it enjoys relations with all except Paraguay and Chile. Trade has increased accordingly. During some years, for example, Costa Rica sells much of its coffee to the Soviet Union, and Argentina much of its wheat. Soviet trade with Latin America amounted to 116.5 million rubles in 1969 and 3,124.4 million in 1981. It continues to rise.[2] In the 1980s, Brazil, Argentina, Peru, Chile, Jamaica, Colombia, Bolivia, Costa Rica, Ecuador, Grenada, Guyana, Mexico, Panama, Uruguay, and Venezuela received aid of one kind or another from the Soviets. The relations between Latin America and the USSR are normal—though, in most cases, quite formal. Washington scrutinizes those relations, testy about the intrusions of another superpower into a hemisphere it still very much regards as its primary sphere of influence.

Washington regards formal relations between Latin America and the Soviet Union as one thing, to be tolerated if not encouraged. Joint Soviet–Latin American denunciations of "imperialism" and any kind of military agreements are quite another, setting off alarm bells in Washington. Latin Americans are wary of setting off those bells. At any rate, they have no particular brief for the Soviet Union. They have few connections with Soviet culture and no attractions to it. The Soviet Union is an abstraction about which few illusions remain.

A problem does arise, however, when, on rare occasions, the Latin American client defies the superpower for whatever reason and, finding no "effective" support—military supplies would be a stellar example—anywhere else, applies to the Soviet Union for it.

When the United States cuts off aid, military or otherwise, to one of its Latin American clients and then tries to block access to European sources as well, it in effect has decided to push the client into a closer relationship with Moscow. This particular action-reaction scenario is by now well played and should offer no surprises. Knowing the scenario well, perhaps Washington replays it in order to prove a point: "See, they were communists all along. We told you so." Certainly whatever link results then permits the ready identification of the Latin American nation as a "security threat," thus ripe for any kind of pressure or intervention. This scenario worked perfectly for Washington in the case of revolutionary Guatemala in the early 1950s. Unable to purchase armaments from the United States and Western Europe, Guatemala, desperate because it feared the invasion of exiles located in Honduras, turned to Eastern Europe in 1954. The arrival at Puerto Barrios of the Polish ship bearing Czech arms heralded the end of the Arbenz government and the Guatemalan revolution. The CIA took the cue for direct intervention. Washington has found the simplicity of that operation hard to repeat in Cuba and Nicaragua, but it has not desisted.

A Soviet threat in the Western Hemisphere, real or perceived, requires the United States, much to its annoyance, to divert attention and forces to a region it would rather take for granted. Nicaragua provides an example. Already the Pentagon has spent billions of dollars building and maintaining a military infrastructure in Honduras and conducting military exercises there as well as off both coasts of Nicaragua. On May 19, 1986, the Pentagon released a report, "Prospects for Containment of Nicaragua's Communist Government," which concluded that an invasion of Nicaragua is the only effective containment. Such an invasion would require at least 100,000 troops, in addition to naval and air power, at a first-year cost in excess of $9 billion.[3] That containment project would diminish the U.S. military presence in other parts of the world. It would divert U.S. attention from other primary areas of security concern.

Planning for the containment or eradication of communism in the Western Hemisphere is a major industry in Washington. One can but reflect on the greater return on the investment if the same time, talent, energy, and money that go into preserving the status quo of institutions promoting social and economic inequities went instead toward economic development whose ultimate result would be a stabler, prosperous, and thus secure hemisphere.

Washington's major concern is not trade, not investments, not repayment of loans, as important as these may be; it is national security. U.S. officials regard major changes of institutions, a declaration of international nonalignment, anti-imperialist rhetoric, and, most particularly, initimate relations with Moscow as a direct challenge—in fact, as a threat—to national security. This perception shapes the world view of Washington, and all the arguments debunking it as paranoia will not alter the vision so long as the official mentality remains constant despite a changing world.

While some of the scenarios of communism engulfing Latin America are extreme, they, nonetheless, reveal an intense and real sensitivity to perceived threats. If Latin Americans are to live harmoniously with their powerful neighbor, they must understand that sensitivity and accommodate it as best as possible.

Well within historical context, the present administration regards the current crisis in its relations with Nicaragua as a consequence of a perceived threat to the national security of the United States. With a differing perspective, others regard the crisis as an opportunity for the United States to adapt to the profound global changes of the last half of the twentieth century and to forge a new, more realistic policy toward the Third World.

The View from the Third World: Nationalism and Development

Obviously the United States and Nicaragua disagree, but Washington has also discovered that Latin America in particular and the Third World in general tend to share the perspective of Nicaragua. They support Nicaragua in world and regional forums. The United States finds itself occupying a minority position, out of touch with two-thirds of humanity.

Nicaragua enjoys wide support for an obvious reason. It is part of the Third World. Though languages, religions, and cultures may fragment the Third World nations, they share in common poverty and most of the same causes for it. They pursue development. In their collective memory fester recollections of humiliating treatment from imperialist countries, old and new.

If questions of security focus the U.S. view, then a concentration on topics of economic development monopolizes the Latin American view. The discussions at the Fourteenth General Assembly of the Organization of American States held in Brasília during November 1984 illustrated those differing emphases. Secretary of State Shultz spoke of Soviet arms shipments to Nicaragua and warned that Nicaragua posed a threat to its neighbors. The audience remained incredulous and unreceptive. Generally supportive of Nicaragua, the Latin Americans admire its plucky challenge of the United States. At any rate, they do not regard Nicaragua as a threat to anyone. They see much bigger threats than that small, impoverished country. In Brasília, they wanted to discuss what they considered to be the "real threat": the debt crisis and its adverse impact on development. Thus, there were two agendas, that of the overdeveloped and that of the underdeveloped, with no integration of them. The official discussions again resembled the dialogue of the deaf.

Whatever form elusive economic development will take in Latin America, as its primary goal it must raise the quality of life for the majority of the Latin Americans, admitting them to some of the benefits of society. Latin Americans generally concur that any major step toward development necessitates the reduction of their economic dependence on Washington. U.S. corporations, the U.S. government, and now U.S. banks determine much of the direction and well-being—or lack of it—of the Latin American economies. Obviously other foreigners invest and loan as well, but the United States still remains the predominant foreign economic power within Latin America.

Partially as a reaction to an overpowering foreign economic presence, Latin Americans rally behind programs of economic nationalism, hoping to use that powerful force as a motor to propel greater national independence and through that independence greater development. Economic nationalism has increasingly characterized Latin America during the last half of the twentieth century. More often than not, the political Left directs it, imposing its ideas and vocabulary. The nationalists have increased the criticism of foreign economic penetration. They accuse foreign investors, companies, and banks of perpetuating Latin America's underdevelopment, thereby contributing to the poverty, ignorance, weakness, and feeling of inferiority of its people. The largest single investor, the United States, is the prime target for much of the nationalist attack. Economic nationalism has called for government control of natural resources, limitations on foreign capital and on repatriation of profits, accelerated industrialization, and trade with all nations regardless of their political or economic ideologies. Furthermore, these nationalists demonstrate ever greater impatience with the ideologies of the past and more interest in experimenting with new ones. The growing force of economic nationalism caused the former Secretary General of the Organization of American States and former President of Ecuador, Galo Plaza, to conclude, "One of the most powerful forces in Latin America today, and one of the least understood outside the region, is the upsurge of economic nationalism." Nationalism is the dominant force within the Third World during the last half of the twentieth century, with every indication of increasing its appeal as the twenty-first century enters.

Nowhere does nationalism pulsate more vigorously than in Nicaragua. Conor Cruise O'Brien made this telling observation: "In John Paul's Poland faith and fatherland have been aligned for centuries, and they still are. In Latin America they have not been, up to now, but in Sandinisimo they are. That is the profound originality of Sandinismo, and the source of much of its power."[4] The interweaving of the power of Sandino's nationalism with the vigor and originality of the popular Roman Catholicism springing from the Christian Base Communities creates an immense and significant new force at work.

Because the United States does not accord Latin American nationalism a sympathetic understanding, it has unwittingly taken on the most potent force in the Third World. Washington detects a Marxian vocabulary it its pronouncements, takes umbrage at its anti-Yankee sentiments, and dislikes its appeal for greater independence of action. A former Guatemalan Foreign Minister, Guillermo Toriello Garrido, observed that the United States confuses Latin America's nationalism with communism. U.S. policymakers, he concluded, labeled

> as "Communism" every manifestation of nationalism or economic independence, any desire for social progress, any intellectual curiosity, and any interest in progressive or liberal reforms.... Any Latin American government that exerts itself to bring about a truly national program which affects the interests of the powerful foreign companies, in whose hands the wealth and the basic resources in large part repose in Latin America, will be pointed out as Communist; it will be accused of being a threat to continental security and making a breach in continental solidarity, and so will be threatened with foreign intervention.[5]

Minister Toriello spoke from experience. The revolutionary government he served came under attack from Washington for exactly those reasons.

It is not difficult to learn what the eloquent nationalist intellectuals want for their societies. They put forth their programs convincingly in print. They claim to speak for the great mass of their impoverished compatriots. They probably do. But to get a more direct understanding of what people want, it is necessary to listen to their voices in the Christian Base Communities, the labor unions, and the rural cooperatives. Their demands seem basic: access to jobs, food, education, health care, and decent housing. Most of the people in developed countries demand these same things—or, more probably, take them for granted. However, since most Latin Americans do not have ready access to them and because they demand access to them, they are actually advocating a profound change in the institutional structures in order to gain access to them. Those institutions inherited from the colonial past and strengthened during the nineteenth century have not addressed, indeed are incapable of addressing, those simple, basic needs.

Many Latin Americans want change. Leading officials in Washington, on the other hand, insist they should be content with the present institutions. The dialogue of the deaf continues. Ambassador Jeane Kirkpatrick, widely regarded as one of the leading ideologues of the Reagan administration, has outlined the benefits of poverty:

Traditional autocrats [those favored by Washington, she affirms] leave in place existing allocations of wealth, power, status, and other resources which in most traditional societies favor an affluent few and maintain masses in poverty. But they worship traditional gods and observe traditional taboos. They do not disturb the habitual rhythms of work and leisure, habitual places of residence, habitual patterns of family and personal relations. Because the miseries of traditional life are familiar, they are bearable to ordinary people who, growing up in the society, learn to cope, as children born to untouchables in India acquire the skills and attitudes necessary for survival in the miserable roles they are destined to fill.[6]

In short, the poor are content thanks to their traditions. Applauding Kirkpatrick's words, President Reagan appointed her United States ambassador to the United Nations, where she could best help the Third World to appreciate the blessings of poverty.

Those who praise "traditional autocrats" and affirm that misery is bearable so long as it is traditional probably cannot understand and certainly will not sympathize with longings for change. Most likely they would find such longings imbued with communist influences. Such a mind-set accepts a "traditional autocrat" like Anastasio Somoza. Certainly the "miseries of traditional life" were "familiar" under the Somozas, and, to follow Ambassador Kirkpatrick's logic, they were therefore "bearable to ordinary people" who learned "to cope" with hunger, disease, illiteracy, and unemployment. Such ideas might pass unnoticed in the nineteenth century, but they have no place amid the quickening pace of challenge and change at the end of the twentieth.

The Nicaraguan people were fed up with "coping" with poverty, traditional or not. They longed for land, health care, education—in short, a decent life. They cast out their "traditional autocrat." To set in motion the powerful forces of nationalism and development, they opted for a revolution. As a result of profound changes, they are on the road to reaching the very goals most people of Latin America—nay, of the Third World—pursue. Pursuing their own goals rather than catering to those of the United States is a novelty for Nicaraguans in the twentieth century. Carlos Fuentes correctly observed, "This is the first Nicaraguan government that acts independently of the United States."[7]

Independence, nationalism, and development, heady concepts of hope in the Third World, do not receive a favorable response from Washington. They forecast change. Washington equates change with challenge and challenge with communism.

IV.
NICARAGUA'S APPEAL AND THE WORLD RESPONSE

The Client and the Superpower

A measure of Washington's—or Moscow's—power is their ability to induce other nations, particularly their client states, to follow their policies. The power can be such that it forces smaller states to behave in ways their best interests do not always counsel. The superpower enjoys great reserves of economic and military strength to permit it to bring tremendous pressure to bear on the client without causing itself any apparent sacrifices, although the client risks monumental sacrifices should it choose to resist the pressure. With limited political and economic options, aware of its vulnerability to pressure, a client state ordinarily seeks to avoid confrontation with the superpower.

On rare occasions, client and superpower clash. Yugoslavia, Albania, Czechoslovakia, and Hungary challenged the Soviet Union in the last half of the twentieth century with varying results. Guatemala and Cuba challenged the United States with equally varied outcomes. If the client is to succeed, it must make the pressures—or the aggression—of the superpower too costly to bear, too inconvenient to sustain.

Deterring the superpower is obviously an overwhelming challenge for any client. To beat the odds, the small state requires both internal and external support. Internally, the government of the small nation must enjoy the enthusiastic support of an overwhelming majority of the population, ready to make whatever sacrifices are required. Further, the government will find it necessary to restrict and to control any opposition minority which would confuse, weaken, or subvert popular resolve, thus increasing the client's vulnerability. Externally, the small state needs allies for psychological, political, and economic support. Optimally, such external support will include one or more large powers whose strength and global objectives conceivably could check the superpower. In the event the superpower decides to apply brute force, the client more than likely will receive no external military support and will be physically defeated, at least in conventional military terms. Those loyal to the defeated government may decide to initiate some kind of a guerrilla war, thereby prolonging the struggle and raising the costs for the superpower.

The small state does enjoy a few advantages in this seemingly one-sided struggle. Its policies and procedures are simplified. Its goals can be quickly reduced to one: national survival. The clear and present danger confers on that goal a vitality and urgency that interlock foreign and domestic policies, evoking all the energies and determination of a people. The danger facilitates the marshaling of all resources. In contrast, the global foreign policy of the superpower complicates its effectiveness. The superpower cannot concentrate all its energies on coercing the client since that objective is but one aspect of a complex international policy. The superpower must balance that conflict with its policies elsewhere, a process that might inhibit its effectiveness, particularly if the conflict protracts.

Psychologically, the small state draws strength from the realization that its survival, or the survival of its independence, is at stake. For the small state, the struggle with the superpower assumes a life-or-death aspect. The unequal struggle between the two inevitably conjures up the David and Goliath comparison, not only increasing national resolve but winning considerable international sympathy as well.

The challenge of a superpower often arouses the courage and dignity of a people—amorphous, yet powerful, attributes. That arousal facilitates the rallying of the citizenry behind the challenged government, diverts attention from domestic problems, and makes acceptable otherwise repugnant hardships and sacrifices.

The time factor could favor either the superpower or the client. If the small nation can count on internal and external support, it can develop a "siege mentality" to its advantage, maximizing its few strengths. It can adapt to the hardships, even learn to use them to its advantage. It develops greater resourcefulness. The inevitable surge of nationalism during a siege further buttresses the client's resolve. On the other hand, a long siege could wear the client down, particularly if supporting nations lose interest and internal pressures rise. Problems exist for the superpower as well. Failure to act resolutely within a brief period to terminate the conflict in its favor might diminish its effectiveness, particularly if the superpower lacks full internal and external support for its actions.

To a large degree, these generalizations apply to the relations between the United States and Nicaragua. Under the Somozas, Nicaragua played the role of a model client state. The revolution of 1979 abruptly altered that role. Rejecting the past, the revolutionaries exhibited greater independence in their foreign relations which, coupled with the dramatic internal changes, brought the once dutiful client state into conflict with Washington. Explanations for the mounting confrontation vary. Washington blames Managua for its intransigence; Managua returns the charge. Whatever the explanations, the historical reluctance of Washington to accept change and the growing demand of Latin Americans for change create an obvious arena of conflict.

Nicaragua's Foreign Policy

While historical amnesia concerning relations with Central America characterizes the citizens and officials of the United States, almost all Nicaraguans are aware of the intrusive role the American government has played in their national history. With that historical consciousness, they understand and, to the extent that past example suggests future action, predict the patterns of present behavior. In short, they use history as an ally. Furthermore, historical knowledge of U.S. interventions and occupations spurs nationalistic sentiments and shapes the present foreign policy. In contrast, ignorant of history, the United States seems willing to repeat it.

Present Nicaraguan foreign policy, while a contrast to that of the Somozas and the compliant governments during the period 1909–1933, has its own historical roots. The taproot is Augusto César Sandino. Throughout the long and difficult guerrilla campaign (1927–1933) to force Washington to withdraw the marines from his homeland, the short, slight, intense Sandino spoke in the name of the Nicaraguan poor. He drew his strongest support from the peasantry. He always identified himself as a son of the people: "I am a city worker, an artisan, as they say in my country.... The elites will say I am a plebeian. Good enough! My highest honor is having come from the oppressed masses who are the soul and nerve system of our race." In addition to his common roots, he stressed his Indian heritage: "I am a Nicaraguan and proud that Indian-American blood, more than any other flows in my veins—blood that contains the mystery of loyal and sincere patriotism." Such identification separated him from the Europeanized elite who accepted and, when possible, profited from foreign occupation.

Sandino believed that the common people alone possessed the strength and honor to redeem the nation: "Only the workers and peasants will fight to the end, only they have the unified force to achieve victory"; and, "Our army is prepared to take the reins of government and to proceed with the organization of workers' and peasants' cooperatives which will harness our natural resources for the good of the entire Nicaraguan family." Sandino preached revolution.

Nationalism was the force both propelling and shaping his struggle and the revolution it promised. The humiliation of a homeland occupied by foreign troops constantly haunted and taunted Sandino. Employing the fiery rhetoric of nationalism, he believed, "It is preferable to die than to accept the humiliating freedom of a slave"; and, "A nation's sovereignty cannot be discussed, only defended with a rifle in hand." Most of his compatriots shared that sense of humiliation as well as the determination to end it. Their lives testified to the growing impoverishment and deepening dependency of their nation under foreign control. They responded to Sandino's nationalistic ardor, which they intuitively shared.

As a testimony to his nationalism, Sandino often repeated that his goals and ideals arose from the Nicaraguan experience, rooted in a past that had known frequent British and U.S. threats, interventions, and occupations. On one occasion he emphasized, "This movement is national and anti-imperialist. We fly the flag of freedom for Nicaragua and for all Latin America. And on the social level it is a people's movement; we champion social justice. People have come here to try to influence us from the international Labor Federation, from the League against Imperialism, from the Quakers. . . . We have always informed them of our basic principle: the struggle is national." Sandino was not a well-read man. His knowledge of imperialism arose from experience, not theory. Likewise, his familiarization with dependency and poverty came from experience and observation, not books. He also had witnessed the Mexican revolution firsthand, and that experience inevitably influenced his thinking. It further convinced him that conditions in Nicaragua reflected broader Latin American patterns.

Although Sandino never summarized his economic, political, and social programs in one document, they are clearly evident in the totality of his writing. He demanded a popular, independent government, the revision of all treaties that limited Nicaragua's sovereignty, and the recovery of the nation's riches and resources for the benefit of all. The Nicaraguan people, he believed, could enjoy a better quality of life only if they had access to the nation's resources, including land, which were owned by the few to the detriment of the many. Although the land should belong to the state, it should be available to everyone: "I believe the state owns the land. . . . I favor a system of cooperatives to work the land." U.S.

occupation had thwarted national development. Pointing to foreign capital and businessmen as a barrier to Nicaragua's prosperity, he encouraged the growth of national industry and commerce. In 1933, he called upon all the nations of the hemisphere to sign a treaty "to outlaw intervention in the internal affairs and to respect the sovereignty and independence of each nation." He pledged his own Army of the Defense of Nicaragua's National Sovereignty to protect the nation from any foreign aggression.[1]

Sandino stated those goals in the broadest, often vaguest, terms. He never elaborated a plan to implement them. He lived to see only one of them realized: the withdrawal of the U.S. Marines signified to him the reestablishment of national independence.

His nationalism, all the more sharply etched because of the U.S. occupation of his homeland, emphasized two principles: national independence and national sovereignty. He dedicated himself to the implementation of those principles, the very foundations on which all Third World movements for self-determination would rest in the last half of the century. Such principles obviously reject "imperialism." Sandino's six-year war against the U.S. occupation force is correctly interpreted as an "anti-imperialist struggle." Believing that the struggle was not just Nicaragua's but that of most of the peoples of the world, Sandino sought international solidarity with his war against imperialism and in favor of self-determination. He realized that alliances with other nations would help to compensate for Nicaragua's weakness. Vice-President Sergio Ramírez locates Nicaragua's present foreign policy firmly within Sandino's guidelines: "There is a similarity between Sandino's ideas and the foreign policy of the Sandinista people's revolution: that of defending their efforts to consolidate the revolution on an international plane through a broad alliance in support of the revolution."[2]

The Historic Program issued by the Frente Sandinista de Liberación Nacional (FSLN) in 1969 contained a section concerning "an independent foreign policy," reiterating Sandino's principles. It called for an end to U.S. "interference in the internal problems of Nicaragua" and the abrogation of all treaties "that compromise national sovereignty," while advocating "a policy of mutual respect

with other countries and fraternal collaboration among peoples."
It welcomed "economic and technical aid from any country, but
always and only when this does not involve political compromises."
The ultimate goal was "to promote ... authentic universal peace."
In 1979, the revolutionary government set about implementing
that foreign policy, in part, as Vice-President Ramírez points out,
"through the Nicaraguan government's membership in the Nonaligned Movement."[3] The historical contrast between two periods,
the late 1920s and the late 1970s, highlights at least one significant
global change over the course of half a century. During Sandino's
struggle nothing even remotely similar to a nonaligned movement
existed.

A group of Afro-Asian nations organized the Nonaligned Movement in 1955 to denounce colonialism, promote economic development, and attempt to relax world tensions. The movement af-
forded international maneuverability to nations that did not want
to be locked into an alliance with either of the two superpowers.
In Belgrade, at the first formal meeting of the movement in 1961,
Cuba was the only Latin American nation to attend. The delegates
emphasized the need for independent foreign policies, advocated
nonparticipation in cold-war military pacts, refused to permit foreign military bases on their territories, supported national liberation struggles, and called for peaceful coexistence. Nicaragua
joined the Nonaligned Movement in 1979, the ninth Latin American member, sending a delegation to the Sixth Nonaligned Summit
in Havana. In early 1983, Managua hosted an extraordinary min-
isterial meeting of the Coordinating Bureau of the Nonaligned
Countries. Delegations from eighty-nine countries, liberation
groups, and international organizations attended. The meeting focused on the Central American crises. The presence of so many
different delegations and their discussions amply demonstrated that
the region was no longer the exclusive concern of the United States
or the Organization of American States. The Nonaligned Movement
supports Nicaragua in its war with the United States. For example,
in late 1984, it once again called for "an immediate end to all

hostile acts and threats" against Nicaragua, reaffirming its support of the Contadora Peace Process.

The Nonaligned Movement continues to attract members from the Western Hemisphere. In 1985, of the 101 members, 18 were Latin American or Caribbean.[4] Despite their obvious diversity, these nations still share what they consider to be unpleasant memories of their relations with a former imperialist power and, above all else, a desire for economic development outside the orthodox communist or capitalist models. Also, the members want to diversify their international relations, including trade patterns as well as sources of aid, investment, loans, and technology.

Reflecting global changes over the course of the last half of the twentieth century, Nicaragua's international experience after 1979 differs from Cuba's after 1959. The Western Hemisphere, under considerable pressure from the United States, had ostracized revolutionary Cuba by the early 1960s. Two decades later, the Latin American countries refuse to repeat that treatment for revolutionary Nicaragua. Nonalignment for Nicaragua has signified the end of dependence on the United States without creating, at least yet, the degree of dependency on the Soviet Union that Cuba was forced to accept in the early 1960s.

Like Cuba, though, revolutionary Nicaragua bears the brunt of U.S. disapproval. The major problem confronting it today is the military presence and pressure of the United States in Central America. In the words of Alejandro Bendana, a high official in the Nicaraguan Foreign Ministry, "We feel threatened by the United States."[5] Just as Nicaraguans perceive their national security is at stake, so do North Americans fear that Nicaragua threatens their national security, not so much by anything the Nicaraguans themselves could do but only if they would permit the Cubans or Soviets to establish military bases on their territory.

Nicaraguans appreciate that fear but probably do not comprehend the depth of it. In an effort to alleviate it, they have made a series of offers to the United States. In April of 1985, for example, President Daniel Ortega offered to call an immediate cease-fire in the war, to ask the United Nations and the Red Cross to help repatriate refugees, to guarantee full freedom of the press, and to reaffirm political pluralism and fundamental freedom. He pledged Nicaragua's commitment to a treaty to ban nuclear weapons in Central America, amnesty for the contras, a prohibition of all foreign military bases in Central America, and the removal of all foreign military advisers. Further, he assured Washington of access to "rigid verification" of the fulfillment of those agreements within Nicaragua. The Contadora Peace Proposal duplicated some of these measures. The State Department refused to talk, let alone negotiate. It stated that these proposals were not new and Managua must negotiate with the contras rather than with Washington.

Later in 1985, the Nicaraguan ambassador to the United States, Carlos Tunnermann, again pursued those proposals. In addition, he pledged that Nicaragua would accept strengthened international verification mechanisms to ensure impartial supervision of compliance with all aspects of the Contadora Peace Proposal. He added that his government had just extended for another year the amnesty law under which all contras, leaders as well as foot soldiers, could rejoin Nicaraguan political life and participate in the framing of a new constitution. Furthermore, he denounced all forms of terrorism, challenging the United States to take its charges of Nicaraguan involvement in such activities to the World Court. The U.S. response remains the same. It routinely classifies the Nicaraguan proposals as "propaganda." President Ortega appeared before the UN Security Council in late July 1986, to plead for peace with the United States. In Chicago, on August 3, he proposed a new treaty of peace and friendship that would recognize the "legitimate security interests of each nation."

The record indicates Washington's repeated refusal to work with Nicaragua to settle outstanding differences. The secret minutes of the National Security Council for October 30, 1984, boasted that the United States had blocked the Contadora Peace Plan. On January 18, 1985, Washington unilaterally suspended the bilateral Nicaraguan–United States talks that had been held in Manzanillo, Mexico, since June 1984. The United States boycotted the World Court, missing an excellent opportunity to prove charges against

Nicaragua. To the request of eight Latin American nations in early 1986 that the United States resume direct talks with the Nicaraguans, the State Department replied, "Reopening bilateral talks now, without any specific moves toward internal reconciliation in Nicaragua, would simply reward the Sandinistas' intransigence. The Sandinistas have no interest in pursuing any settlement that would jeopardize their control. They have no interest in genuine democracy. . . . Our position is that the first thing they ought to do is open a dialogue with [the contras]."[6]

To the Nicaraguans, the repeated refusals substantiate their conclusion—and fear—that Washington is wed to a military solution. It only awaits the proper moment for military intervention. In the broader historical perspective of Washington's relations with Latin America, the obduracy and the willingness to impose force follow traditional patterns. That they persist is explicable, but whether they will still be effective at the end of the twentieth century is questionable.

Meanwhile, Nicaragua pursues a nonaligned foreign policy to which many Latin American nations respond affirmatively. The latter would like to redefine their relationship with Washington, although at far less cost than Nicaragua has had to pay. They appreciate the attraction of the Nonaligned Movement, in their eyes a viable alternative to dependency on the United States. Perhaps it can serve as an intermediate step, "diversified dependency," toward greater independence. Since the traditional exporting economies and dependency of the past have not brought about the economic development they seek, the Latin American nations eye the New International Economic Order with some hopes that it might benefit them more, permitting them a "third path," complementary to the nonaligned option Nicaragua has selected. The Nicaraguan example is more appealing, at least theoretically, than the Cuban. In that sense, Nicaragua appears vaguely as a new alternative whose experience will offer valuable lessons.

Thus far, two conclusions seem certain. First, nonalignment has ended Nicaragua's dependence on the United States. Although Nicaragua may be on the road to greater independence, no one doubts that the journey will be long and hard. Second, whatever antagonisms exist, the best interests of Managua dictate a close trading relationship with the United States. Its absence handicaps Nicaragua. An accommodation thus far has eluded the former client and superpower to the disadvantage of both. Such an accommodation would signify no surrender for either party. It acknowledges historical reality: 1987 is not 1927. One measurement of the difference is that while Sandino received scant international support in his struggle, the global community has accepted the Nicaraguan revolution, sympathized with its aspirations, and supported its goals.

World Response

In early 1929, Sandino sadly noted:

We are all alone. The cause of Nicaragua has been abandoned. Our cause outside Nicaragua has been weakened by a lack of communication, a lack of spiritual exchange that sustains our struggle here in Nicaragua. In addition, U.S. dollars are buying people and influence in order to restrict the flow of our information to the outside world. This isolation is doing us a great deal of harm.

A half century later, Nicaragua's struggle with the United States continues, but the world no longer indifferently averts its eyes. To an impressive degree, it responds positively to Nicaragua's plight. That response fathers action.

Like Sandino, his spiritual heirs understand the importance of international support. Minister Tomás Borge concluded:

[International] solidarity is the most elevated expression of the revolution. ... We see that the peoples of the world, through their own organizations, trade unions, political parties, and other associations, the populations of Latin America, North America, Europe... can put certain limitations on his [Reagan's] desire to inflame all Central America.[7]

Minister of Agriculture Jaime Wheelock told delegates to the First

International Conference in Solidarity with Nicaragua in early 1981, "Your presence here has a deep revolutionary significance— both of internationalism and solidarity—because it amounts to a show of support from the whole world."[8]

Amid all the post-1979 tribulations, isolation was the last thing Nicaragua had to fear. In 1977, Somoza maintained diplomatic relations with fifty-two nations; today the revolutionary government has relations with nearly one hundred. In much of the world, the name of Nicaragua has become practically a household word. It finds its way, day after day, onto the front pages of the newspapers. Books and articles about Nicaragua cascade off the presses. The revolution, its program, its achievements, Washington's unremitting hostility, and the war awaken world sympathy with and interest in that small and hitherto unknown country.

Forlorn Managua hosts the world. Through its small international airport pass statesmen, politicians, and intellectuals from every continent. Probably no month has gone by in which Nicaragua was not the seat of some international congress. Volunteers from around the globe arrive to harvest crops, build houses, staff clinics, teach technological skills. International volunteers participating in the 1985 coffee harvest, for example, constituted a virtual mini–United Nations. They came from the United States, Canada, Mexico, Guatemala, El Salvador, Costa Rica, Panama, Colombia, Chile, Bolivia, Argentina, Libya, Cyprus, the Netherlands, Switzerland, Denmark, Norway, Austria, France, Spain, Greece, Germany, Czechoslovakia, and the Soviet Union.

The tense struggle for change and survival has attracted rather than repelled tourists. Curious to see a revolution in motion, more than 100,000 foreigners visited Nicaragua in 1985, fully 40 percent of them from the United States. Tourism ranked fifth as a foreign-exchange earner and employed directly or indirectly twenty-five thousand people.[9]

The trade statistics (see table on page 103) for the first half of the 1980s suggest the global extension of Nicaragua's reach. With the exception of Cuba, the trade with Latin America contracted; with the United States it halted after Reagan imposed the embargo;

**Structure of Nicaraguan Foreign Trade—Exports and Imports
(Percentages by Region)**

	1980	1984	1985	1986*
Central America	28.1%	9.2%	6.8%	7.4%
Latin America	13.5	12.8	8.5	7.1
United States	30.4	14.9	7.3†	0
Western Europe	17.6	25.2	28.0	37.7
Eastern Europe	1.0	15.4	28.8	27.2
Japan	3.0	9.9	7.7	9.0
Canada	2.6	2.9	1.6	2.4
Cuba	—	4.0	4.4	4.2
Others	3.8	5.7	6.9	5.0
	100.0%	100.0%	100.0%	100.0%

*Forecast.
†January–May 1985.
Source: Nicaraguan Ministry of Foreign Trade.

but with Europe—Eastern and Western—it expanded impressively. Exports to the United States had been declining since 1955, when they totaled an impressive 65.2 percent, falling to 28.8 percent by 1977, and to zero in 1986. Trade with Canada and Japan remains firm.

The combination of arrogance and ignorance shaping U.S. policy in Central America has alienated the Latin Americans and worked to Nicaragua's advantage. Latin American attitudes toward the United States spring from a historical wariness of the "Colossus of the North." All Latin American governments anxiously watch the U.S. military support of a dissident faction, the materialization of a nightmare that haunts them. Throughout history, none of the nations has escaped "invasions" of these types of dissidents—some threatening, others of a more opera buffa aspect, but all taken seriously by always-nervous governments in power. Political tenure in Latin American can be precarious. Any outside attack, most particularly when Washington's participation can be seen, has been and will be interpreted as an attack on national independence, national institutions, even national existence. No Latin American leader can afford to support such an attack. Regardless of ideology, the governments tend to unite in their opposition to Washington's meddling in Latin American affairs, a reality abundantly evident to everyone except Washington. Such meddling constitutes an alarming security threat. Each government realizes that it might just as easily be under Washington's pressure; each understands that the domestic force of nationalism might incite powerful opposition to any government legitimizing Washington's meddling. The claims made by Secretary of State Shultz that the Latin American governments back the U.S. war against Nicaragua evinces either pure bravado or ignorance, one more indication of the intellectual isolation of Washington.

At this moment in Latin American history when democracy has made a truimphant return after decades of military dictatorships, the new democratic governments realize their fragile institutions require peace not just to strengthen themselves but to continue to exist. War in Central America complements militarism, a dominant historic characteristic the democracies are trying to control. It also creates an adverse economic climate. The combination of war, increased militarism, growing tensions, and economic stagnation could affect the stability of all Latin America. It threatens nascent democracy. The Latin American leaders are acutely aware of the dangers, although Washington seems oblivious.

Democratic Latin American leaders speak out consistently to favor the Contadora Peace Process, to oppose U.S. intervention, and to condemn the contras—in short, to favor peace. President Alan García of Peru declared, "We support Nicaragua because it is a symbol of sovereignty and the continent's independent destiny. We do so unconditionally."[10] He warned, "If it [the United States] doesn't change, the U.S. will have to face in a few years a bunch of hostile governments in the region."[11] Before a joint session of the Argentine Congress, he stated, "Every aggression against Nicaragua would be considered an aggression against all Latin America," and added that Peru "would break relations with the aggressive power and do everything in its power in defense of the brother country." Thunderous applause greeted his remarks.[12] The president of Argentina himself, Raúl Alfonsín, has been no less emphatic and candid. On several occasions, opposing aid to the contras, he has urged

President Reagan to open a dialogue with Nicaragua, to chart a peaceful course in Central America. His voice forms part of a Latin American chorus:

Our point of view is based on the principles of self-determination, non-intervention and support for the work of the Contadora group. We need a political solution in Central America. The issue is a complicated one for all the democratic countries of Latin America, even those farthest from the area, because it is one that polarizes societies. We cannot cast aside the security of the region for the security of the U.S. We must not have interference by any extracontinental power. We must avoid the idea that anyone can interfere in any given country.[13]

Former President Carlos Andrés Pérez of Venezuela has also warned that Latin America would rise up in indignation if the United States invaded Nicaragua. President Belisario Betancur of Colombia has taken up the same themes, foremost of which is his search for peace in Central America: "We consider it urgent to halt the arms race, to forbid intervention in the area in all its manifestations and to prevent actions aimed at destabilizing the governments of the region."[14] He emphasized, "A military response is a non-policy. Central America requires political and diplomatic solutions, not military ones."[15]

Actions accompany those words. The Latin Americans work hard to return peace to Central America. Solidly unified, they advocate an end to all aid to the contras and the implementation of the Contadora Peace Plan. Venezuela, Colombia, Panama, and Mexico initiated that peace process after their meeting in January of 1983 on Contadora Island off the Pacific coast of Panama. Their plan calls for the removal of all foreign military personnel from Central America, a phased reduction of all military forces in the region, strict border supervision to protect the sovereignty of each state, verification, and democratic pluralism with free elections. In July of 1985, Argentina, Uruguay, Brazil, and Peru formed the Contadora Support Group in an effort to push forward the peace process. The eight nations whose governments represent 85 percent of the population of Latin America met in La Paz, Bolivia, in early August

1985; later that August in Cartagena, Colombia; and in Carabelleda, Venezuela in January 1986. Each time they appealed to Washington to support the Contadora Peace Plan, to terminate aid to the contras, and to resume negotiations with Nicaragua. In February 1986, the foreign ministers of those eight nations traveled to Washington to personally urge President Reagan to heed these appeals. They expressed the oft repeated fear than any invasion of or intervention in Nicaragua could have a politically explosive effect throughout Latin America. They visited Washington because in the eyes of these Latin Americans, the major obstacle to peace in Central America is the Reagan administration.[16] Washington curtly dismissed each appeal.

Latin America backs Managua in a variety of ways. Many of the governments extend credit and loans. Mexico has been particularly generous with credit. A few send technical experts. Brazil, for example, announced in mid-1985 it would send agricultural and industrial advisers. Moral support abounds. The appearance of Nicaraguan leaders in Latin America always draws large, vociferous crowds. When Daniel Ortega visited Rio de Janeiro following his election to the presidency, the mayor handed him the keys to the city, proclaimed Rio to be a "sister city" of Managua, and declared, "Your cause is not only the cause of Nicaragua but of the Third World and Latin America."[17] While Ortega was in Montevideo in early March of 1985 to attend the inauguration of President Julio María Sanguinetti, tens of thousands of Uruguayans poured into the streets and jammed the main downtown plaza in front of his hotel to greet him. On another occasion, in Buenos Aires, when Argentine singer Susana Rinaldi interrupted her performance to announce the presence of Vice-President Ramírez, the entire audience of the Teatro Colón rose to give a standing ovation that lasted several minutes.

At a very formal hemispheric level, Nicaragua enjoys the support of the Organization of American States. Cognizant that the OAS charter prohibits its members—including, of course, the United States—from using force to overthrow the government of another member state, its General Assembly in 1983 and again in 1984 passed resolutions favoring the Contadora Peace Process. Isolated within that organization, the United States no longer brings before it any matters related to Central America.

Professor Hewson A. Ryan, Murrow Professor of Public Diplomacy at Fletcher School of Law and Diplomacy at Tufts University, has concluded, "The reasons the United States has not had recourse to the [OAS] system are as obvious as they are tragic. The United States is more politically isolated in the hemisphere than at any time since President Polk ordered troops into Mexico in 1846, or since Teddy Roosevelt 'took' Panama. At the OAS, we would be hard pressed to find two or three votes to support the U.S. posture on Nicaragua."[18]

This isolation contrasts with the former ability of the United States to muster endorsement from the OAS members for just about anything. In 1954, Secretary of State John Foster Dulles extracted an OAS resolution against Guatemala to complement U.S. intervention. In the early 1960s, the OAS stood firmly with the United States in the Cuban missile crisis. The membership complied with the U.S. request to boot Cuba out of the organization. In 1965, when President Lyndon Johnson intervened in the Dominican Republic, he carefully involved OAS Secretary General José Mora and members of a special OAS commission in a favorable resolution of support. Apparently such maneuvers are no longer possible. Although hardly hostile to the United States, the OAS is no longer its pliant tool. It seems to have abandoned its original role of giving unqualified support to superpower policy. Alejandro Bendana of Nicaragua's Foreign Ministry commented, "Usually it is the United States that marshals Latin America to its side. This time, the tables are turned."[19]

Unlike previous presidents, Reagan does not speak of the inter-American system or evoke the OAS charter. The message has gotten though to him that Latin Americans reject his policies. He admitted in February of 1985 that the United States would use force in Central America only as a last resort because of Latin American opposition to intervention: "Our own friends and allies south of the border and the OAS would not tolerate our going in with armed force in Latin America."[20]

The Organization of American States, created in 1948, no longer functions to anyone's satisfaction. In effect, the United States has withdrawn. Murmurs among Latin Americans reveal their discontent. The Malvinas (Falkland Islands) War, accompanied by the Central American crises, drove home to them the fact that the OAS in its present form does not, possibly no longer can, serve their interests or even speak to their concerns. Some voice the historic hope of an organization without U.S. membership.

The reality the Reagan administration does not, perhaps cannot, grasp is that Latin Americans fear the nearby, ever-present, and all-powerful United States much more than they do the distant Soviet Union which has never bombarded any of their ports or occupied any of their countries or conspired to overthrow any of their governments. It is not the Soviet Union but the United States they fear as it expands its role in a regional war that brings death, destruction, economic collapse, and instability to their doorsteps. Summing up Latin American opinion, Carlos Fuentes concluded, "Ronald Reagan has done the United States the greatest disservice in Latin America by reminding everyone where the danger comes from. We will not cry 'uncle.' "[21]

Economic realities play a determinate role in Central America. Economic collapse, not Nicaragua, constitutes the major problems for each of the governments. During the period 1950–70, the Central American economies virtually were without debt, inflation, fiscal deficit, or monetary instability. The 1970s witnessed a drastic change. The Central American foreign debt rose from $564 million in 1970 to $18 billion in 1985. Fiscal deficits leaped 1,000 percent during the decade of the 1970s. As of 1986, the real per capita income for Guatemala and Costa Rica has fallen to 1972 levels; for Honduras, to 1972; and for El Salvador, to 1960.[22] While the figure for Nicaragua is 1965, it can be misleading for a Socialist economy in which the "social wage" of free education, health care, and access to land; rent control; and subsidized prices for all basic items have not been figured. By 1986, the United States subsidized the economies of El Salvador, Honduras, and Costa Rica in sums of millions of dollars per day, making those governments increasingly beholden to Washington.

Exerting formidable influence over Honduras, El Salvador, and Costa Rica, the United States does not hesitate to apply pressure on those weak states to accommodate its Central American policy. Even so, those governments manifest a noticeable ambivalence rather than the enthusiasm Washington would like.

Although often quarreling among themselves, the nations of Central America exhibit a certain degree of unity—some of it theoretical, no doubt—which pervades the region. The Central American Common Market illustrates the consensus that only greater integration can provide the economic viability necessary for development. Industrialization demands it. An expanding transportation network and vastly improved communications weld the five states more closely together. In short, closer relations exist among the five Central American states than the international press might lead one to conclude. The Central American economist Xabier Gorostiaga observed, "I don't think Reagan understands how integrated the Central American nations are, nor how transnationalized the region is today."[23] Despite Mr. Reagan's embargo, Nicaragua trades with the other Central American states. The only impediment to greater trade with them is Nicaragua's lack of ready cash.

Innocent of Central American historical and geopolitical realities, Washington has given preference in its policies to Honduras, brushing aside Guatemala. By ignoring its historically preeminent role in the region and failing to work within a well-estblished power hierarchy, Washington probably offended Guatemala and nudged it closer to Nicaragua. Guatemala, whether under the former military dictatorship or the present formal democracy of the courageous President Vinicio Cerezo, has maintained correct relations with Managua, favoring the Contadora Peace Plan and criticizing aid to the contras. Like his predecessors, Cerezo proclaimed, "We do not sympathize with any policy of aggression against any country of Central America."[24] Foreign Minister Mario Quiñonez Amezquita bluntly stated that Guatemala "does not support the policies of the president of the United States against Nicaragua."[25] In May of 1986, President Cerezo convened all five Central American presidents at Esquipulas, Guatemala, the first such summit since the Nicaraguan revolution, to issue a joint declaration of intention to sign a regional peace treaty drawn up by the Contadora nations and to create a permanent Central American parliament. An opponent of the contras, he criticized Reagan when he learned the United States planned to spend $100 million on them. For one thing, he was indignant that Washington would spend $100 million to subvert the Central American economies and only $40 million in support of the fledgling democracy in Guatemala.

Harper's published a poll in early 1986 showing that 40 percent of the Costa Ricans thought Nicaragua interfered "too much" in their internal affairs but that 50 percent thought the United States did too, some indication of which nation the Costa Ricans believe poses the greater threat to them. Much as Costa Ricans would like to turn their backs on the Central American crises, they realize they are inevitably mired in them. Former President José Figueres expressed some of the frustrations the Costa Ricans feel:

If the United States wishes to change the government of Nicaragua, let it send its own troops to do it instead of asking farmers from Costa Rica and Honduras to go and die on the borders. To us it seems wrong that a great power should financially contribute to the slaughter now taking place; it also seems wrong that the United States should not respect the way of thinking of the governments of other nations.[26]

Some Costa Ricans salute the neighboring revolution, while others abhor it. In common, all of them want Costa Rica to be left alone, an impossible wish.

Contras under the leadership of Edén Pastora took refuge in northern Costa Rica and for several years carried on hit-and-run guerrilla forays into Nicaragua. President Reagan pressures Costa Rica to play an active role in the war to defeat the Sandinistas. Still, the Costa Ricans seek to escape the morass. In February 1986, Costa Rica and Nicaragua signed a significant border agreement, supported by eight Latin American nations to establish a "permanent force of inspection and vigilance" charged with keeping peace along the border. The agreement set an important precedent for contemporary Central America.

A depressed economy makes Costa Rica prey to Washington's economic pressures and rewards. Reagan's special envoy to Central America, Philip C. Habib, was supposed to have admonished Oscar Arias for criticizing Washington's support of the contras. The newly elected president was told he was embarrassing President Reagan and warned it could cost Costa Rica much-needed economic aid.[27]

After his inauguration, President Arias toned down his comments, perhaps to avoid embarrassing Mr. Reagan, while at the same time he has implemented a policy favoring peace in Central America. He has vowed to keep Costa Rica out of the conflict and to facilitate a negotiated settlement. The border with Nicaragua remains quiet. Pastora has "retired," at least for the moment. The contra presence dwindled to nearly nothing. Seemingly a major cause for possible Costa Rican involvement has been removed.

On Nicaragua's northern border, the situation for Honduras is even more complex, reflecting perhaps its greater poverty, underdevelopment, and dependency, and its desperate need for whatever funding can be obtained from the United States. Honduras has served the United States as a launching pad for invasions before, into Guatemala in 1954 and into Cuba in 1961. Now, Washington pressures it to play a similar role for the invasion of Nicaragua, and officials in Tegucigalpa are only halfhearted. In an interview poll with two hundred political, labor, peasant, and religious leaders during March and April 1986, journalism students of the National University found that 179 opposed the presence of the contras in Honduras, while only 16 favored it; that 157 opposed Honduran aid to the contras, while 20 approved; that 151 believed Washington decided Honduran foreign policy, while 25 concluded the Honduran military did, and 24, the Honduran government.[28] While officials cannot afford to offend the United States, they really do not want to antagonize Nicaragua.

For the long run, Honduras appears to be in serious trouble.

None of the aid, at least thus far, has contributed to development. The country's plasticity in the firm hands of Washington has earned it an unenviable international reputation as the archetypical "banana republic." Meanwhile, the United States has reinforced and strengthened the army of its real rival, El Salvador; helped to fill vulnerable, underpopulated frontier regions with an unpredictable and certainly an uncontrollable contra army; and raised the level of distrust of its increasingly powerful southern neighbor, Nicaragua, not to mention the level of suspicion from the usually preeminent northern neighbor, Guatemala. Of the five Central American nations, Honduras has most seriously lost control of its own destiny. Although the immediate destiny of Honduras is to march to the drummer of the American government, many express uneasiness and hope for a better future.

President José Napoleón Duarte of El Salvador has lost whatever internal support he might have enjoyed. The military and elites have always opposed him, reluctantly accepting him as chief executive only because Washington insisted and because he serves as the conduit for the required and desired U.S. aid. His middle-class, labor, and peasant support has disappeared amid civil war and economic collapse. Indications in 1987 are that less than a quarter of the population endorses his presidency. Ever more dependent on Washington, President Duarte has been reduced to the role of its Central American mouthpiece. The world acknowledges that reality. His former international esteem has long since evaporated. Largely because of its prolonged civil war, the El Salvador of Duarte has become more dependent on Washington than has Honduras, and, hence, is the least ambivalent of the Central American governments that Washington manipulates.

If Latin America in general proves hostile to U.S. policies and Central America in particular proves ambivalent, Washington is having just as much difficulty persuading its northern neighbor to endorse them. Ottawa's foreign policy toward Nicaragua contrasts sharply with Washington's. It originates from quite a different perspective of events. Prior to 1979, with scarcely any contact with that republic, Canada concentrated its attention on the Commonwealth nations of the Caribbean, leaving Central America to the domain of Washington. The Nicaraguan revolution and the ensuing Central American crises have changed all that. The Department of External Affairs now regularly issues position papers on Nicaragua and Central America.

The government of Prime Minister Pierre Elliott Trudeau shaped the present policy, and when the Progressive Conservatives replaced the Liberals in power after the September 1984 election, speculation existed as to which direction Prime Minister Brian Mulroney would take. Or, would he just forget Nicaragua? If anything, his government has strengthened Canada's presence in Central America and friendship toward Nicaragua. Indicative of the high level of Canadian interest and continuity of policy, two Secretaries of State for External Affairs have visited Nicaragua: Allan J. MacEachen in 1984 and Monique Vezina in 1985.

Secretary of State for External Affairs Joe Clark disagrees openly with Washington's policies. He criticizes aid to the contras and cautions against U.S intervention. In deference to diplomacy, he gingerly phrases it, "The Canadian Government opposes third party intervention in Central America."[29]

The vote in the U.S. House of Representatives on June 25, 1986, to allocate $100 million for the contras evoked somewhat stronger diplomatic language from the Secretary: "The ... congressional decision to provide additional aid to the contras runs counter to our position. Canada has constantly emphasized its firm belief that the countries of Central America must be free to seek their own solution to their own problems without interference from any outside source." A few days later, Canada applauded the judgment rendered in favor of Nicaragua by the International Court of Justice, or World Court.[30]

Above all else, Canada actively backs the Contadora Peace Process. That support springs from the belief shared by the Liberals and Progressive Conservatives alike that Central America's problems have been created by historic social and economic forces and can only be solved by changes in the region's social and economic institutions. Canada despairs of any military solutions. Therefore, the first item on any realistic agenda to resolve the crises must be the reestablishment of peace. As have the past Secretaries of State for External Affairs, Mr. Clark vociferously endorses the efforts of the Contadora nations. He has conferred with them singly and jointly. In the name of Canada, he endorsed the Declaration of Carabelleda, the statement of the Contadora nations and the Contadora Support Group of January 1986, asking for an end to aid to the contras and the resumption of peace talks in Central America.[31]

Canada provides guidance on the security and control aspect of the Contadora Peace Plan, suggesting its willingness to join a control and verification commission. In a position paper on the Contadora process, the Department of External Affairs stated, "We very much hope, of course, that Canada would be able to back the eventual agreement by signing a Protocol which would imply political and moral support to the peace process in Central America." Secretary Clark emphasizes, "The need for a comprehensive agreement and for a workable and effective verification process remains urgent and essential."[32] In the 1980s, Canada obviously has become an active participant in the Central American dramas.

While Canada envisions its primary role as a force for peace, it plays other roles as well. It furnishes aid. Only after the revolution did Canada's bilateral development program with Nicaragua begin. Between 1981 and 1986, Canada contributed over $50 million (Canadian) in direct aid and international humanitarian assistance to Nicaragua.[33] Private Canadian groups, such as Tools for Peace, have contributed more than $3 million (Canadian).

Canadian technicians participate in the Momotombo II geothermal electrical project, to which France and Italy also contribute. If Nicaragua could but harness its vast geothermal potential, many of its critical energy problems would be solved. Canadian volunteers participiate in every activity from coffee picking to staffing hospitals.

Like the rest of the world, Canada opposed the embargo. At the same time, Canadians regard it as an opportunity. One official of the Department of External Affairs in May 1985 greeted President Reagan's announcement of the U.S. embargo with a practical assessment: "The fact that the U.S. is out of the market means that there is room for everyone else." Vowing that Canadian businessmen will sell Canadian goods to Nicaragua as substitutes for U.S. products blocked by the embargo, Secretary Clark openly disagrees with Washington's trade embargo: "I explained our skepticism that the policy they [the U.S. government] are following will achieve the goals that they have set and might achieve opposite goals."[34]

Canada exported $22.5 million (Canadian) in goods to Nicaragua and imported $45.3 million in 1984. Those figures more or less represent the export flow from Canada to Nicaragua for the five-year period 1981–85, the low being 1982 ($15.6 million) and the high 1984. Canada's import record varies more radically, the low being 1982 ($26.6 million) and the high 1981 ($52 million). An agreement signed in 1946 still governs trade between Nicaragua and Canada.[35]

After Reagan imposed the embargo, Managua moved its North American trade office from Miami to Toronto. Due to that embargo, Canadian shipments to and from Nicaragua via the United States had to be discontinued. Much of the trade between the two nations had followed that route. Canada and Nicaragua continue to explore new shipping routes to invigorate their trade. Canadian businessmen, indeed the Canadian government itself, are anxious to pursue the promise of greater commerce. The major obstacle seems to be Nicaragua's shortage of foreign exchange. Meanwhile, the crises focus Canadian attention on Central America, particularly on Nicaragua, to an unprecedented degree.

Active interaction with the Central Americans denotes a major policy shift on the part of the Europeans, too, putting Washington on notice that they intend to play a role in that part of the world so long reserved for and by the United States. Europeans sympathize with Nicaragua. They understand the need, even urgency, for change. Mass street demonstrations from Athens to London, Oslo to Madrid, denounce U.S. policy and express European concern. When President Reagan arrived in Madrid on May 5, 1985, massive street demonstrations greeted him. The embargo on Nicaragua, imposed just days before his visit, angered the Spaniards, exacerbating resentments of the presence of U.S. bases on Spanish soil. As part of their protest, the hundreds of thousands of marchers held copies of *El País*. That influential newspaper carried the results of a poll reporting that 64 percent of the Spaniards surveyed did not believe either Reagan or the U.S. were sincere friends of Spain, that 74 percent thought Reagan's defense policies hindered the quest for peace, and that 66 percent wanted a reduced U.S. military presence in Spain. In sum, Spaniards doubted the wisdom of an alliance with the United States. The U.S. treatment of Nicaragua focused their distrust and anger.[36]

Europeans were doing more than venting their disagreement in the streets. The governments of Western Europe initiated a novel program of aid to Central America. In September 1984, ten foreign ministers of the European Economic Community (EEC), joined by Spain and Portugal, met in San José, Costa Rica, with their five Central American counterparts. Just prior to their meeting, Secretary of State Shultz had written the Europeans to discourage them, urging that "region-to-region assistance not lead to increased economic aid or any political support for the Sandinistas."[37] The Europeans followed their own agenda. They recognized that the crises in Central America arose from the institutionalization of dependency, underdevelopment, and poverty—causes divorced from the East-West conflict. They determined to increase economic aid to the region without discriminating against Nicaragua. Denouncing the use of force as a means to solve the crises, they demanded the end to the "foreign military presence in Central America" and pledged support to the Contadora Peace Plan. Finally, they called for stronger economic ties between Europe and Central America.

During the November 1985 meeting in Luxembourg of twenty-one foreign ministers of the EEC, the Central American nations signed their first political agreement with the Europeans. It endorsed economic cooperation, the removal of all foreign military elements, and active opposition to terrorism. It reiterated the belief that "social injustice and economic imbalance are largely to blame for the political instability in Central America."[38] The EEC and the Central American nations agreed to hold annual meetings.

The joint action within the EEC did not eliminate programs of aid and support from individual European countries. Most of them generously funnel funds to embattled Nicaragua. Despite the fact that France succumbed to U.S. pressure to terminate military aid, Paris continued to offer economic help to Nicaragua. Between July 1979 and September 1984, France granted Nicaragua over $213 million in aid, 65 percent of which constituted donations toward economic development. On another level of support, in March of 1985, the French government awarded the Order of Arts and Letters to Minister of Culture Ernesto Cardenal. The poet-priest is one of a group of only twenty non-Frenchmen who have received that honor.

Only Prime Minister Margaret Thatcher keeps silent amid growing European criticism of Reagan's Central American policies. The opposition Labor party, on the other hand, rallies behind the Sandinistas, promising to add material and military aid to moral support once it returns to power. In mid-1984, all three major British political parties—including, obviously, Mrs. Thatcher's own Conservative party—issued a joint statement calling on the White House to stop supporting the contras.

The U.S. policy toward Nicaragua drives a wedge between the United States and its European allies, causing some to fret that it weakens the NATO alliance. Senator Christopher Dodd, Democrat from Connecticut, expressed the problem before Congress in these terms:

What I think has occurred ... is that not only do we have a conflict with Nicaragua, but that we find ourselves in the middle of May of 1985, four years after the initiation of the contra operation, in a situation where we are confronted with a two-front conflict, a conflict not only with the Nicaraguans but also now we find ourselves in conflict with our European and Latin American allies.[39]

In many ways, the crisis of confrontation between the United States and Nicaragua exposes the isolation of the United States that extends far beyond the Western Hemisphere. Headlines in the *New*

York Times of March 29, 1983, pithily told the tale: "US Finds Itself Virtually Isolated in UN over Nicaraguan Crisis." The United Nations faithfully reflects the trend. The United States consistently has lacked support for its Central American policies, while, just as consistently, Nicaragua has enjoyed an overwhelming majority of votes in its favor in both the Security Council and the General Assembly.

Nicaragua savored a major diplomatic triumph over the United States in October 1982, when it decided to run for one of the nonpermanent seats on the UN Security Council reserved for Latin America. The United States backed the Dominican Republic. Nicaragua, endorsed by the Arab Group, the African Group, and the Nonaligned Nations—among others—won the required two-thirds vote of the General Assembly to hold a key international position for two years. In March of 1983, Nicaragua focused the attention of the Security Council on the CIA's not-so-secret war in Central America. During four days of debate, the United States remained isolated in its effort to portray the conflict as an internal Nicaraguan affair. In October of 1984, the UN General Assembly passed a resolution holding that the Contadora Peace Plan provided the basis for peace and the promotion of economic and social development of the region. A more thorough reading of the UN voting records only strengthens the conclusion that Nicaragua enjoys global support in the world's most important forum.

While contributing to and further involving itself in the already inherent, historical crises in Central America, Washington has failed to formulate a positive policy to resolve them. The deepening of the crises and certainly their protraction have brought Central America to the attention of the world. Europe, Canada, Latin America, other Third World countries, Japan, the Soviet Union, the Socialist nations, and now the People's Republic of China pay much more attention to that small, once-neglected region of the globe than ever before. Their interest and concern have ended its isolation and in the process diminished U.S. domination. The Central American crises are no longer the exclusive concern of the United States. Whatever remained of the force and power of the Monroe Doctrine has dissipated. The Latin Americans and Europeans understand, even though Washington has not quite got the message, that the fortunes of the Western Hemisphere are no longer subject to only one power. In the future, Central America will never again fit into Uncle Sam's pocket.

Whether President Reagan will "lose" Nicaragua on his "watch" still remains to be seen, but more significantly he already has lost the exclusivity of U.S. power in the Western Hemisphere declared by James Monroe in 1823 and imposed after the Spanish-American War of 1898. As Carlos Fuentes phrased it, "The real political choice for the United States in this hemisphere is between the contras and the governments of Latin America."[40] Reagan chose the contras. The Pax Americana no longer extends unquestioned throughout the Western Hemisphere.

V.

NICARAGUA,
THE UNITED STATES,
AND A NEW WORLD ORDER

The Challenge to Pax Americana

America's isolation in its war against Nicaragua reveals how much the world has changed within the span of the last half of the twentieth century. If not exactly over, the Pax Americana retains little of its former vigor and encounters increasingly effective constraints.

The United States emerged victorious from World War II, the only world power whose economic infrastructure remained intact. It had amply proven its military might. In the dawn of a new era of peace, it alone possessed the most awesome weapon of any arsenal: the atomic bomb. In those heady years of triumph, power, and optimism, the United States created a new world order, the Pax Americana, the organization and ordering of the world in accordance with an American vision. It championed the goals of rational international intercourse and peace. In a weakened world, the strong United States acted through the international organizations it established, guided, and, to a large measure, financed: the United Nations, the World Court, the Organization of American States.

A serious flaw, less noticeable in the decade after World War II but increasingly apparent ever since, existed: the model exclusively mirrored American views. Noble as some of those views might have been, all could not reflect the desires of a complex world. The brute reality, which Americans do not always understand, is that much of the world has its own visions, understandings, hopes, and goals. Often they do not harmonize with the American model, and sometimes they clash with it. Other peoples, not so sure that America always knows best, feel better served by their *own* aspirations.

In that decade after the war in which the Organization of American States served as a more useful institution for U.S. policy in Latin America than the State Department, in which the membership in the United Nations rose from fifty-one to seventy-four while still maintaining a predominantly European and Western Hemispheric composition, and when no country would dream of bringing the United States before the World Court, America pretty much got its global way, even though in American eyes the emergent Soviet bloc appeared like a menacing cloud on an otherwise sunny day. As a commentary on its times, National Security Council Document Number 69 appeared in 1950. While calling for a "firm policy ... to check and roll back the Kremlin's drive for world domination," it advocated at the same time "a world environment in which our free society can survive and flourish." That, in fact, was the goal, the reason for being, of the Pax Americana. A strong military combined with a vigorous economy to make the Pax Americana possible, at least momentarily. The United States employed its economic preeminence, its proven military strength, international law, and the international organizations it had created to impose its Pax Americana.

Once the Soviet Union, with its own formidable military establishment, began to recover economically from the devastating effects of war, the Pax Americana faced its first major challenge. The United States had never welcomed the communists into power. World War II momentarily had driven the two nations into a mutually beneficial alliance. The defeat of Nazi Germany ended the need for it. The differing economic and political systems of both giants did not exist comfortably side by side. The Soviet explosion of an atomic bomb in 1949 and successful launch into the heavens of Sputnik in 1957 confirmed Washington's allegiance to the new alliances it had formed: the Inter-American Treaty of Reciprocal Assistance (Rio Treaty) in 1947; the North Atlantic Treaty Organization in 1949; the tripartite security pact with Australia and New Zealand (ANZUS) in 1951; the Southeast Asia Treaty Organization (SEATO) in 1954. The United States also associated closely with the Baghdad Pact (1955), later renamed the Central Treaty Organization (CENTO, 1959), after Iraq withdrew, leaving Turkey, Iran, Pakistan, and Great Britain as members. Washington belonged to the economic, military, and countersubversion committees of CENTO. At the time, that vast network of treaties buttressed the power of the United States, contained the Soviets, and promised to perpetuate the Pax Americana. The treaties demonstrated Washington's early acknowledgment that the Pax Americana required cooperation from friendly states if it was to be enforced effectively. Likewise, the treaties suggested international acquiescence in the reality of the Pax Americana.

Although most attention has focused on the rise of Soviet power as the challenge to Pax Americana, other global changes increasingly and probably inevitably limited its reach and continued effectiveness. Europe's remarkable economic recovery in the late forties and early fifties reestablished its prominence, increasing its independence. The People's Republic of China emerged in 1949. Japan became a major financial, commercial, and industrial power. The Third World and the Nonaligned Nations were international realities by the 1960s. The increasing temptation of détente attracted more and more nations as a sensible way of reordering international alliances, priorities, and behavior to better insure peace. The defeat of the United States in Vietnam after a long, costly, and divisive war exposed its vulnerability, the formal sign of what most of the world had earlier anticipated: the United States was no longer the impregnable giant. Too many changes and too many challenges had made that unique position untenable.

By the end of the 1960s, the United States was losing control of those very international institutions it had created to project its power. The United Nations increasingly attracted the attention and participation of the Third World. In the General Assembly, those nations did in fact enjoy the legal equality they avidly pursued. As Third World nations came to outnumber others in the United Nations, the United States was less able to marshal votes in its favor. The voting record of 1984 illustrated the independence of action of those nations. The Arab states voted with the United States in only 1 out of every 10 issues; the African states, 2 out of 10; the Asian and Pacific nations found a compromise—1.5 out of 10. Mexico opposed the U.S. position 90 percent of the time. Egypt, the second largest U.S. aid recipient, voted 87.5 percent of the time against the United States.[1] State Department officials glumly admitted that the United States failed to win votes in that international forum and offered this reasoning: "We have seen in the United Nations . . . how international organizations have become more and more politicized against the interests of the Western democracies."[2] The other side of that coin might reveal that those nations no longer found that the United States or the "Western democracies" served their best interests. Subscribing to one or another manifestation of nationalism and the desire for development, they pointed to their deepening poverty and then to the prosperity of the "Western democracies" to indicate that Western leadership had not benefited them.

By the seventies, it was all too apparent that the United States no longer controlled the world economy. Japan challenged U.S. economic predominance. To further compromise its global leadership, Washington wrestled with the legacy of the Vietnam experience: reluctance on the part of most Americans to fight wars in the Third World. This reluctance complicates the U.S. response to the challenge of change in Nicaragua.

Unwilling or unable to find new policies for the last decades of the century, Washington has reached back to midcentury to resurrect those policies it employed successfully in Guatemala in the early 1950s, despite their obvious inapplicability to the times and temper of the 1980s. True, the United States did invade Grenada in 1983 and militarily topple the government, putting in place one more to its liking. Grenada seems to constitute a special case. A mini-nation only 133 square miles in size with a population of barely 100,000, it is approximately one four-hundredth the size and one thirtieth the population of Nicaragua. Tiny Grenada possesses no resources to defend itself against anyone and certainly not against the most powerful nation in the world. Apparently in order to gain the support of the U.S. public for military operations, the target must meet at least four standards: it must be limited and focused in scope, have a clearly defined enemy, be capable of speedy resolution, and result in few casualties. The Grenada operation met those standards. A "quick," "clean" victory, the invasion thrilled Americans.

Any operation in Nicaragua would not fit those standards. Although by no means large—Nicaragua is approximately the size of North Carolina—it is definitely not a Grenada. It would take many times more than the six thousand troops that landed in Grenada for a Nicaraguan operation. The ratio of U.S. troops to the population of Grenada was one to seventeen. If one applied that same ratio to Nicaragua, 175,000 troops would be required. But one must bear in mind that Grenada had no army to speak of, no defense worthy of the name. Nicaragua has an effective, battle-trained army and militia, with an armed population to boot. Despite the best efforts of the Reagan administration to define the "enemy" in Nicaragua, Americans remain uncertain who it is. Issues remain murky, and Americans are loath to enter a foggy fray. In fact, American public opinion has been and remains overwhelmingly opposed to war in Nicaragua.

The military itself is cautious about Nicaragua, realizing the costs of such an invasion, finding the lack of public support an ill omen for another foreign adventure, and fearing the sapping of its strength in other regions the officers consider more vital to U.S. security. General Wallace A. Nutting, Commander of Army and Air Force Combat Forces in the United States, voiced those reservations. He harbored no illusions about an invasion: "Overthrowing the Sandinistas would be a major operation, requiring multiple divisions and air support and sea support to go along with it. There would be a big fight to dislodge them." Apparently his views echo those widely held among senior military officers and reflect statements made by the Joint Chiefs of Staff to President Reagan and the Secretary of Defense.[3] For other reasons discussed in this book, Nicaragua necessitates considerably more risk to invade than Grenada, with little hope of either a "clear" or a "quick" victory and every expectation of protracted guerrilla warfare that could inflame all of Central America. General Manuel Antonio Noriega, Commander in Chief of Panama's armed forces, warned, "Military aggression against a Central American country would become a region-wide conflict."[4] Adding its voice to the chorus of protest against any intervention, *El Dia* of Mexico City also insisted that such an action "would regionalize the war."[5]

Yet, with little fuss and hardly a second thought, the United States did intervene in Guatemala back in 1954 to cast out constitutionally and democratically elected President Jacobo Arbenz and replace him with Colonel Carlos Castillo Armas, who never competed in an election and only confirmed himself in power with a yes-or-no plebiscite. A comparison and contrast between the intervention in Guatemala in 1954 and the war in Nicaragua in the 1980s highlight the changes that have occurred in the world and certainly in Latin America during the last half of the twentieth century. Very importantly, the United States firmly controlled the United Nations in 1954 and prevented any Guatemalan appeal from being heard in that forum. Further, it manipulated the OAS so thoroughly that it arranged a resolution endorsed by the Latin Americans condemning Guatemala. Guatemala stood alone, effectively isolated from outside support, even moral support. The government depended on an army which the revolution had not restructured. Its loyalty was at best questionable. In 1954, it refused to defend the revolution.

The CIA operated with impunity. It organized, equipped, and financed an exile army in Honduras. That ragtag army, even though it did invade Guatemala in mid-June of 1954, did not overthrow the government. CIA planes bombed Guatemala City and five other cities, creating a psychological panic. A terrorized and disloyal army refused to follow the orders of President Arbenz. U.S. Ambassador to Guatemala John Peurifoy accompanied Castillo Armas to Guatemala City in a U.S. plane and installed him in office. In a radio address to the American public on June 30, 1954, announcing the changes in the Guatemalan government, Secretary of State John Foster Dulles declared, "The events of recent months and days add a new and glorious chapter to the already great tradition of the American States." One cannot be sure if the statement was a master stroke of cynicism or satire.

Participants in the 1954 intervention in Guatemala have reacted differently to the U.S. war in Nicaragua. A young Nester Sánchez served as U.S. liaison officer with the Honduran military in 1954. In 1986, he is Deputy Secretary of Defense for Inter-American Affairs, and his statements echo those of three decades ago. He sees in the CIA success in Guatemala a model operation to be duplicated in Nicaragua. Philip C. Roettinger, a retired Marine Corps colonel who played a role in the defeat of Arbenz, looks upon the current CIA efforts to unseat Ortega with different eyes:

I now consider my involvement in the overthrow of Arbenz a terrible mistake, one that this Administration seems bent on reenacting in Nicaragua. . . . When I authorized Castillo Armas, then in a Tegucigalpa safehouse, to return to Guatemala and assume the presidency that we had prepared for him, I had no idea of the consequences of the CIA meddling. Our "success" led to 31 years of repressive military rule and the deaths of more than 100,000 Guatemalans. Furthermore, the overthrow of the Arbenz government destroyed vital social and economic reforms, including land distribution, social security and trade-union rights. . . . The coup that I helped engineer in 1954 inaugurated an unprecedented era of intransigent military rule in Central America. Generals and colonels acted with impunity to wipe out dissent and garner wealth for themselves and their cronies. . . . I am 70 years old now. I have lived and worked in Latin America for more than 30 years. Done with skulduggery, I devote my time to painting some of the region's beautiful scenery. It's painful to see my government repeat the mistake in which it engaged 32 years ago. I've grown up. I only wish my government would as well.

He concluded that "aid to the Nicaraguan contras is repeating Eisenhower's tragic error."[6]

No issue disturbs Latin Americans at the end of the twentieth century more than U.S. intervention. Their compliance in the interventions in Guatemala in 1954 and the Dominican Republic in 1965 and their willingness to ostracize Cuba in the 1960s haunt them. Once again, the articulate Carlos Fuentes best captures the Latin American determination in the 1980s to serve their own cause and not that of the United States:

We Latin Americans have an identity. We know our place in the world better. Things now are certainly not as they were 30 years ago, when Jacobo Arbenz was overthrown in Guatemala without a murmur in the United States and with only a feeling of helplessness in the rest of the hemisphere. If, let's say, Nicaragua were to be invaded by U.S. troops, for instance, you'd see all of Latin America rising up in great anger. I don't think the United States really understands what it would mean to have a whole continent rise against it. Yet, this is very possible. Oh yes, I am quite serious. Should there be a U.S. invasion of Nicaragua, it would offend the Right and the Left throughout the hemisphere. Now, I am convinced that nationalism is the area where the Right and Left coincide in Latin America. If you don't believe me, think of how this was demonstrated in the war of the Malvinas, the Falklands. And if Nicaragua were invaded, this time you would see young Argentines, Peruvians, Colombians, and Mexicans rushing to Central America to fight there. Against the marines! Against the contras! We would see international brigades. Like in the Spanish Civil War.[7]

As vocally as the Nicaraguans, the Latin Americans condemn the mining of the harbors, criticize the undeclared war, call for the negotiated settlement as put forth by the Contadora nations. Together they challenge a superpower they believe is out of touch with the times and out of step with the rest of the hemisphere.

The Pax Americana does not suit the temperament of the Latin Americans at the end of the twentieth century. It certainly does not serve their goals. Their behavior within the OAS reflects their mood. As they distance themselves from Washington, they unite more closely among themselves, isolating the United States.

The Pursuit of Global Unilateralism

Reviving the 1954 Guatemalan scenario in order to apply it to Nicaragua is but one manifestation of Washington's preference for the policies of the past. Conceivably an even older model exists: the U.S. intervention in Nicaragua in 1909 to unseat President José Santos Zelaya and the subsequent occupation of that country for more than two decades. As events in the 1970s and 1980s in Central America demonstrate, those interventions resolved little. The region is probably more bereft of social justice, more inflammable, more hostile to the United States because of them. Clearly underdevelopment, dependency, and poverty still predominate. No reason exists to believe that one more intervention will resolve any of the basic social, economic, and political problems that agitate the isthmus, deepening its instability and arousing U.S. security concerns.

The real preference for the past, however, lies in the misty memories of the Pax Americana, a part of the politics of nostalgia. Arnold Toynbee coined the term "Shadow Empire" to describe the behavior of a once-omnipotent world power in decline, frustrated, intent upon recapturing past glories. The term carries some relevance today for a Washington resurrecting the rhetoric, beliefs, and policies not just of a defunct Pax Americana but of an even earlier era when it commanded the destinies of Central America completely.

Washington's policies toward the Third World generally have sprouted from the ideas that the United States can and should dominate most of that vast region and, furthermore, knows what is best for it. Those ideas have changed less over time than the realities of a Third World increasingly embittered by persistent poverty, dependency, and underdevelopment; increasingly nationalistic and assertive; and increasingly hostile to tutelage. Slowly Third World leaders have acknowledged that the dominant nations seldom serve the best interests of their client nations. Slowly they have come to appreciate the truth of the words of the U.S. envoy to Managua in 1926, Lawrence Dennis. He frankly summarized the U.S. position in occupied Nicaragua: "Here people often think we come to serve the interests of one lot against the other, but they're wrong. We serve our own interests." History amply illustrates that any dominant or hegemonic nation serves itself first. At best, the Third World nations can expect to benefit tangentially, if at all, from their relationship with the more powerful state. Third World elites, and most recently members of the fragile middle class, who fear change often ally themselves with the superpower in an effort to perpetuate their own benefits. That minority and its military establishment provide cover for the penetration and control of the superpower. Together, they have thus far deterred economic development to favor sporadic economic growth.

Such an alliance between the Third World elite dependent on Washington to retain or to regain its privileges and power and a Washington determined to exercise its control can be graphically seen in the numerous newspaper photos of a jovial President Reagan surrounded by the obsequious Calero, Robelo, and Cruz. Because snapshots of the master and the minions fuel the flames of nationalism, they are widely reproduced in Nicaragua in deference to the old Chinese adage that a picture speaks a thousand words.

President Reagan more than any of his recent predecessors frames his rhetoric and policies within the belief that American global power must be absolute in the final decades of the twentieth century. To that belief, the ability of the United States to impose its will on Central America is absolutely essential. Washington regards Central America as its primary sphere of influence; any display of independence, any defiance of U.S. control there cannot be tolerated. To paraphrase Reagan, how can the United States expect—or be expected—to exert its authority anywhere else in the world if its authority is questioned or defied on its very doorstep? So tenacious is that belief within the Reagan administration that it has sacrificed its authority and goodwill elsewhere in its determination to bring Nicaragua to heel.

In order to put the Humpty Dumpty of absolute American power back together again, the Reagan administration glues together the restoration of America's military supremacy through the Strategic Defense Initiative ("Star Wars"), the domination of the Third World proclaimed in the Reagan Doctrine, and the dismantlement or disregard of the multilateral arrangements, international organizations, alliances, and international law that Washington now perceives as impediments.

The Reagan Doctrine shapes all U.S. relations with the Third World. Fundamentally it opposes change, fearing that such change opens the door to Soviet entry. For as long as possible, for example, it supported, then tolerated, Ferdinand Marcos in the Philippines and "Baby Doc" Duvalier in Haiti. When the overthrow of each became inevitable, Washington helped to choreograph elaborate departures of the tyrants. In both of these cases the dictators left, but the fundamental institutions on which they fed and on which pervasive poverty in those two lands also feeds, remain intact. Where are the sweeping agrarian reforms that the Philippines and Haiti must have in order to take the first step toward development? These cases illustrate that Third World leaders are expendable for Washington, but the institutions on which they thrived are not.

The Reagan Doctrine opposes any perceived Soviet advances into Asia, Africa, and Latin America by offering military aid and counterinsurgency training to anti-communist governments, a policy that often aligns the United States with some unsavory characters. The doctrine also includes the formation and/or support of guerrilla movements to challenge governments judged to be too Marxist, too pro-Soviet, or just plain unfriendly to the United States. Under this doctrine, the CIA has supported guerrilla movements in at least eight different countries, among them Afghanistan, Cambodia, Angola, and Nicaragua. The involvement is heaviest in Central America where the United States is at war with Nicaragua.

To carry out this doctrine in Nicaragua, as throughout the world, the Reagan administration must turn its back on alliances, treaties, international law, and international organizations. It must do so because all of these cite many of the U.S. actions as illegal. There is a moral condemnation as well. Thus, the Reagan administration sees as barriers in the 1980s the very institutions its predecessors created in the 1945–55 period to implement international supremacy of the United States.

The NATO situation is particularly significant because for three decades the United States has considered that premier alliance as fundamental for national security. More often than not, the United States has gotten its way within NATO. Yet, the United States has allowed its policy toward Nicaragua—and other matters such as the bombing attack on Libya—to threaten, perhaps to weaken, the alliance, as the Europeans favor the Contadora Peace Plan and oppose aid to the contras. Providing material aid and moral support to Nicaragua, they tend to view events there as efforts of a Third World country to develop. They perceive the struggle in Nicaragua as one to replace iniquitous institutions with fairer ones rather than as yet another battle in the seemingly endless East-West conflict. Obviously such views clash with Washington's. Sharply divergent viewpoints disrupt NATO harmony.

The Council on Foreign Relations issued a sober report in March of 1985, "Third World Instability: Central America as a European-American Issue," warning that increasing tensions between Washington and the Western European governments over U.S. policy in Central America could seriously weaken NATO. The report pointed to the sharp criticism of U.S. policy by Spain's Foreign Minister Fernando Moran. He warned that direct intervention by the United States in Central America would force Spain to withdraw from NATO. Further, he pointed out that in Europe the results of a direct U.S. intervention would be to "strengthen neutralist and pacifist movements to such an extent that it could jeopardize the continued participation in NATO of some of its members, especially Spain." Moran cited "substantial resistance" emerging throughout Western Europe to the U.S. treatment of the crises as a manifestation of the East-West conflict. Stressing his country's special relationship with Latin America, he concluded, "Spain's views on Central America can have some degree of influence on other, less-concerned European governments." Although favorable to U.S. policies, Alois Mertes, the second-ranking official in the West German Foreign Ministry, fretted, "Were Central America to distract the United States psychologically, politically, or militarily from the focal point of the Soviet threat and of Western security—namely Europe—the consequences for the cohesion of the Atlantic Alliance would be incalculable."[8] Long before the report of the prestigious Council on Foreign Relations focused attention on a possible crisis within NATO, Europeans had expressed and discussed their concern that Reagan subordinated NATO to other objectives. David Watt, the former director of the Royal Institute of International Relations, concluded that as a result NATO may be "Reagan's real victim."[9] Now that European concern deepens, West German Minister for Economic Cooperation Juergen Warnke, after an August 1986 trip to Latin America, declared that a U.S. invasion of Nicaragua would be a catastrophe devastating to the Western alliance.[10]

Secretary of Defense Caspar W. Weinberger has acknowledged that the Central American crises strain the NATO alliance: "It causes strains. There's no question about it." He admitted that he spends a considerable amount of time trying to reassure NATO allies about U.S. policies in the isthmus.[11] General Wallace Nutting bluntly concluded, "If we invade Nicaragua, not only will we jeopardize working relationships with the hemisphere but we will with a bunch of our NATO allies as well."[12]

NATO may be the primary but it is not the sole example of floundering alliances. CENTO is dead, buried, and forgotten. SEATO is little more than an ideological memory. The ANZUS meeting in 1986 consisted of Australia and the United States with the notable and embarrassing absence of an old ally, New Zealand. Rather than try for accommodation, the United States let a quarrel with New Zealand over the visiting rights of nuclear-powered and/or nuclear-armed ships rupture the ANZUS treaty organization in 1985. The rupture illustrated that an alliance with the superpower can offer the small state more liabilities than benefits.

At odds with the Latin American governments over its treatment of Nicaragua, Washington ignores the Organization of American States, deeming it no longer useful, certainly no longer "dependable." Nor does Washington invoke the 1947 Inter-American Treaty of Reciprocal Assistance because there is every reason to suspect that the United States is violating it. Under that treaty, "an armed attack by any State [hemispheric or extrahemispheric] shall be considered an attack against all the American States and, consequently, each one of the ... contracting parties [shall] undertake to assist in meeting the attack." Might not some government argue that the contras are in part the creation of the United States and thus implicate the United States in an attack on Nicaragua? Such questions could employ an army of lawyers to resolve. Washington, understanding it stands on swampy legal ground, prefers to ignore rather than evoke a treaty which one of the leading scholars of inter-American relations, J. Lloyd Mecham, characterized as "in a very real sense, the capstone of the inter-American security structure."[13]

If alliances can be ignored then so, too, can treaties and international law. The United States signed a host of treaties forbidding intervention, and the Constitution mandates that treaties are a part of the "supreme Law of the Land." To carry forward the Good Neighbor Policy of President Franklin D. Roosevelt, the United States entered into a series of treaties with Latin America in the 1930s, foreswearing any future intervention. The incredulous Latin Americans treasured them. In the Convention on Rights and Duties of States (1934), Article 8 read, "No state has the right to intervene in the internal or external affairs of another"; Article 11 affirmed, "The territory of a state is inviolable and may not be the object of military occupation nor of other measures of force imposed by another state directly or indirectly or for any motive whatever even temporarily." Should any doubts linger about intervention, the Additional Protocol Relative to Non-Intervention (1937) would seem to dissipate them with its clear language: "The High Contracting Parties [of which Nicaragua and the United States were two] declare inadmissible the intervention of any one of them, directly or indirectly, and for whatever reason, in the internal or external affairs of any other Parties." The United States and Nicaragua signed the United Nations Charter and the Organization of American States Charter, both of which proscribe any kind of interventions for any reason. For example, Article 20 of the OAS Charter mandates, "The territory of a state is inviolable; it may not be the object, even temporarily, of military occupation or of other measures of force taken by another state, directly or indirectly, on any grounds whatever." One could also point out appropriate sections of the 1956 bilateral treaty of friendship between Nicaragua and the United States. For example, the embargo imposed by President Reagan violated the treaty provisions then operative for "freedom of commerce and navigation" between the countries. These treaties do not address the interests of the Reagan administration, which at best ignores them and at worst violates them.

The administration's treatment of the International Court of Justice, popularly called the World Court, offers the most mischievous example of U.S. disregard for international law. Nicaragua as a small state relies on international law. In fact, because of their weakness, most nations of the Third World sanctify the rule of law, the principal means by which they enjoy equality with larger, more powerful states. Any retreat from the rule of law disturbs the Third World. A prominent Third World ambassador to the United States explained, "From the point of view of the middle and little countries, the current U.S. retreat from internationalism is a bad thing. Our interests are jeopardized when there is a decline in the rule of law and if the greatest power in the world retreats from the system."[14] International law strengthens international order. Together they guarantee the independence of nation-states against those who might use superior military strength to impose their will.

The United States has celebrated the importance of international law throughout this century. It helped to create the World Court, the judicial arm of the United Nations. In a persuasive speech, John Foster Dulles argued the importance to the United States of the World Court:

If the United States, which has the material power to impose its will widely in the world, agrees to submit to the impartial adjudication of its legal controversies, that will inaugurate a new and profoundly significant international advance. Conversely, a failure to take that step would be interpreted as an election on our part to rely on power rather than reason.[15]

The United States accepted the compulsory jurisdiction of the Court in a declaration deposited with the United Nations on August 6, 1946. That declaration provided that upon six months' notice, the United States could cancel that acceptance.

Washington loyally served the court for nearly forty years in the challenging task of substituting law for force in international conduct. The United States made its last appearance before the Court in 1980 during the Iranian hostage crisis. Iran, for its part, refused to submit to the Court's jurisdiction, evoking U.S.—and international—condemnation for its decision. At that time, Attorney General Benjamin Civiletti lauded the Court, the representation of "the highest legal aspirations of civilized man."

Discovering in early 1984 that the CIA had mined its major harbors, Nicaragua immediately introduced a resolution into the UN Security Council calling on the United States to cease and desist. A U.S. veto blocked the resolution. The Nicaraguans then decided to take their case against U.S. intervention to the World Court. On April 6, 1984, just three days before Nicaragua filed suit, Washington, having caught wind of what was about to happen, attempted to frustrate the case by announcing that it would not accept the compulsory jurisdiction of the Court over any Central American questions for two years. The maneuver violated the commitment to the requirement to give a six-month notice before withdrawal.

At any rate, Nicaragua proceeded on April 9 to file suit in the World Court, petitioning it to order the United States to stop all support of the contras, mining of its harbors, and "military and paramilitary" aggression. It also filed a claim against the United States demanding compensation for damages caused by aggression. The Court responded on May 10; while a final decision on the complaint of aggression was being considered, it called on the

United States "to fully respect Nicaraguan sovereignty and political independence" and to "immediately cease and refrain from any actions restricting, blocking, or endangering access to or from Nicaraguan ports, and in particular, the laying of mines."

To the U.S. charges that the International Court of Justice lacked jurisdiction in this case, the Court responded on November 26, 1984, by rejecting by a vote of fifteen to one the argument that the United States had removed itself from jurisdiction and by a vote of sixteen to zero the argument that the Court was not competent to hear the case. The Court agreed to hear it and reaffirmed its May order directing the United States to end its aggression against Nicaragua. *Time* termed the decision "a clear rebuke to the United States."[16] Judges from countries intimately allied with the United States—Great Britain, France, West Germany, Italy, and Japan—voted against Washington and in favor of Nicaragua. A dilemma faced Washington: whether to risk defeat in the World Court or to ignore the court and violate the very international law it accuses Nicaragua of trampling in its alleged support of the Salvadoran rebels.

On January 18, 1985, the United States announced its withdrawal from the case, the first time it had ever withdrawn from a case before the World Court. The precedent disappointed world opinion. After all, just a few years earlier, the United States had ridiculed Iran for its refusal to go to the Court concerning the question of the hostages. Four years later, a major world power that had prided itself on its devotion to the rule of law and on its support of the Court followed Iran's example. It created the impression that the United States was unwilling to defend its actions in Nicaragua, confirming for many their worst suspicions of U.S. activities in Central America.

The case proceeded without the presence of the United States, just as the U.S. case in 1980 had gone forward without the presence of Iran. The International Court of Justice ruled on June 27, 1986, that U.S. support of the contras violated both "customary international law" and a 1956 Nicaraguan–United States friendship treaty. By a vote of twelve to three, the judges ordered the United States to cease that support, and by a fourteen-to-one margin ruled that it must compensate Nicaragua for economic losses incurred in the conflict. The Court also rejected a U.S. claim that support of the contras constituted collective self-defense on the part of the United States and other Central American nations against Nicaraguan aggression; ruled that training, arming, financing, and supporting the contras breached the U.S. obligation under international law not to intervene in the affairs of another nation; held that the United States violated Nicaraguan sovereignty and countered international laws prohibiting the use of force against another state; and found the U.S. embargo and mining of harbors violated the 1956 Nicaraguan–United States Treaty of Friendship, Commerce, and Navigation. Finally, the judges urged both nations to subscribe to the Contadora Peace Process. Sitting on the case, judges from countries tied to Washington through three major alliances—NATO, ANZUS, and the Rio Treaty—voted against the United States, reemphasizing its isolation from its once-closest allies.

Denying the jurisdiction of the court, the United States refused first to plead its case and then to accept the rulings. State Department spokesman Charles E. Redman explained. "The court is simply not equipped to deal with a case of this nature involving complex facts and intelligence information. We consider our policy in Central America to be entirely consistent with international law. Nicaragua is engaged in a substantial, unprovoked, and unlawful use of force against its neighbors. The United States has assisted the victims' response to Nicaragua's intervention." Other officials affirmed that the war formed part of a regional problem beyond the Court's scope and that Nicaragua masqueraded propaganda as a legal case. The State Department already had stated that Nicaragua, Cuba, and the Soviet Union were subverting the World Court by turning it into a political weapon.[17]

Reaction to the Court's ruling outside of official Washington differed considerably. Nicaraguans, of course, savored their legal triumph. Foreign Minister Miguel D'Escoto, saluting the judgment as "the best guarantee" for peace in Central America, urged the United States to accept it:

We hope that today's judgment will have a sobering effect on the Reagan Administration. As a result, we hope that the United States will choose to join the law-abiding nations of the world, honor its international commitments, desist from its policy of covert wars and respect the sovereignty of all nations regardless of size.

He concluded that the refusal of the large power to accept the Court's decision would "tarnish, perhaps irreparably, the trustworthiness of the United States as a responsible member of the international community."[18]

Editorial opinion in the U.S. press concurred that the United States had violated the charters of the United Nations and the Organization of American States as well as international law. The refusal of the Reagan administration to accept the Court's judgment only magnified its significance. The *Christian Science Monitor* called the World Court decision "a smashing diplomatic defeat for the United States."[19] The Los Angeles *Times* soberly noted, "Citizens of the United States, so committed to a rule of law, can take no satisfaction from this turn of events, in which their nation has chosen brute force rather than the legal instruments of redress to confront a crisis in the region. The rule of law is the weaker for that, and the United States is no stronger."[20]

Questions inevitably arise as to how well served the United States is by ignoring the Court. The United States refused to entrust its case to the World Court; and when Nicaragua did, Washington refused to defend its own policies and position before the justices. One need not be a sophisticated international lawyer to apply the treaties as well as international law and customs to U.S. behavior in Central America and conclude that the U.S. policy toward Nicaragua is unlawful. Later in the UN Security Council, the United States vetoed a resolution reaffirming the authority of the Court and calling on all nations to comply with the decision of the Court and to refrain from any political, economic, or military action that might impede the peace efforts of the Contadora nations. The resolution did not mention the United States by name. The U.S. Ambassador to the United Nations, Vernon A. Walters, stated that the United States had vetoed it because it "could not, and would not, contribute to the achievement of a peaceful and just settlement of the situation in Central America."[21] The world not only questions whether the U.S. case is just but also whether it is logical.

Whether just or logical, the policies of Washington have been consistent. They ignore the United Nations and the Organization of American States as well as the World Court. The United States declined to take its case against Nicaragua to either the UN or the OAS for two very good reasons. Its actions in Central America violate the charters of both organizations. Furthermore, Washington could count on few of the members of either organization to back its position. Ironically, while much of U.S. behavior in Central America springs from an oft expressed concern that the international community will believe it unable to keep its commitments, that very community, particularly the Third World, witnesses the failure of the major power to abide by international law, including its treaty agreements.

The support of the United States for international law unravels during the Reagan administration, a contrast with the traditionally strong emphasis placed on international law throughout U.S. history. Although not always observed in practice, international law always commanded rhetorical allegiance. In addition to the foregoing evidence concerning Reagan's disregard for international law, his administration also refused to sign the 1982 Law of the Sea Treaty, negotiated bipartisanly in Congress and signed by 156 nations, or even to cooperate in the revision of six of the four hundred articles to which Washington objects. It has unilaterally reinterpreted the 1972 Antiballistic Missile (ABM) Treaty to facilitate the development of the "Star Wars" program. It has delayed ratifying two 1979 protocols to the 1949 Geneva Convention on combatants and war victims. Its record of establishing the legal premises for military adventures is weak. In Grenada, Lebanon, Libya, Angola, and Central America, its explanations of how the United States complies with international law furrows more brows than it soothes. Daniel J. Scheffer, a lawyer and formerly an international affairs fellow of the Council on Foreign Relations, characterized them as "skimpy, tardy and unpersuasive."[22]

To fight odious international terrorism, apparently any law can be broken, which the seizure of the Egyptian airliner carrying the hijackers of the *Achille Lauro* exemplified. President Reagan's inclinations toward unilateralism surfaced in his comments on the U.S. planes forcing the Egyptian plane out of international airspace and onto an Italian landing field: "We did this all by our little selves." The Independent Commission on Respect for International Law took a less sanguine view. It characterized the Reagan years as "a period during which the United States has moved decisively from being a champion of law and internationalism to being an abettor of old-fashioned unilateralism that refuses to be tied down by legal restraints, that treats laws like fences, made to be climbed."[23]

The willingness of the United States to stand alone in the world manifests itself in other ways. The charges hurled against the World Court that it has become a political weapon are also aimed at the United Nations and the United Nations Educational, Scientific, and Cultural Organization. The U.S. withdrew from UNESCO, claiming it had become "overly politicized," a code word used with increasing frequency to indicate criticism of the United States or the posture of a nation or organization acting in an independent fashion which does not complement U.S. positions. The Third World now dominates UNESCO and has for more than a decade. The "overly politicized" voice grating on official U.S. ears is actually the discussion of two-thirds of humanity, the expression of their views, and the articulation of their hopes. Since these voices within UNESCO do not harmonize with the ideas or even the ideals of Washington, officials denigrate them as "political" or "ideological," apparently unaware of the fact that the Third World classifies those of the United States in exactly the same way.

The United States, a generous contributor of fully a quarter of the UN budget, has served notice that it will reduce that sum by 20 percent. Some Reagan officials express outrage that the United States contributes so heavily to subsidize critics and to provide them with a perfect platform for their criticism. One former legal adviser in the Reagan administration remarked, "It's not 1946, when everyone thought the UN would save the world. So what does the United States do—continue to hope and pray that standards will be followed, when they're not, or are there areas that require re-analysis?"[24] Possibly one of those areas for reanalysis may be the existence of the UN itself or continued U.S. participation in it. As the United States discovered in its crisis with Nicaragua, the UN hinders more than it helps Washington's policy. The UN which turned a deaf ear to Guatemala's cries for help in 1954 listens attentively and sympathetically to Nicaragua in the 1980s, the surest possible sign that the Third World dominates the general Assembly and influences the Security Council, somewhat more removed from Third World influence because of the veto system. That these international organizations no longer exclusively serve the United States intensifies Washington's pursuit of global unilateralism.

Pax Americana arose to fill an international political and economic vacuum in the years immediately following World War II. The economic recovery of Europe and Japan; the military, technological, and economic strengthening of the Soviet Union and much later of the People's Republic of China; the emergence of the Nonaligned Movement; and the political cohesion of the Third World, all contributors to the growing complexity of international relations, eventually challenged that single supremacy. Ironically, the very international institutions created to facilitate the Pax Americana proved, in time, to be major challenges to it.

Nicaragua after 1979 represents the goals of the Third World: the effective exercise of sovereignty, independence, and self-determination. Actually, the UN Charter of Economic Rights and Duties of States summarized those aspirations: "Every State has the sovereign and inalienable right to choose its economic system as well as its political, social, and cultural systems in accordance with the will of its people, without outside interference, coercion or threat in any form whatsoever." If, indeed, these goals are to be realized, then the major powers must adjust to new international realities limiting their influence and maneuverability.

Nicaragua presents a case study of the difficulty of one of the superpowers, the United States, in accepting the international realities of the last decades of the twentieth century. Contrary to the advice of its allies, in opposition to its treaty obligations, in violation of international law, without the support of either the UN or the OAS, the United States has chosen to challenge the change and in effect attempt to reverse history by force and through unilateral action. Rejecting international law and organizations, the Reagan administration offers little to replace them except military force. Foreign policy shifts from the State Department to the Defense Department and particularly to the CIA. The obsession with Nicaragua drains attention and energy from larger and certainly far more important problems such as the impending economic collapse of Latin America and the declining efficacy of NATO.

During the heyday of the Pax Americana, Washington could count on the international cooperation or acquiescence of much of the world. When that cooperation diminished as goals diverged, the United States hesitated to accommodate the changes abroad in the world. That failure of accommodation propelled it along the path of global unilateralism, putting it increasingly at odds with the rest of the world.

The obsession with Nicaragua and the unilateralism of a "Shadow Empire" bode ill for world order and stability and, ultimately, for U.S. security. In the meantime, diminutive Nicaragua bears much of the brunt of the U.S. challenge to change.

Challenges to change recall the pertinent historical judgement made by Will and Ariel Durant, authors of the widely acclaimed, multivolume historical survey *The Story of Civilization*. They capped their long and productive careers with a slender tome based upon their joint observations of the past. Appropriately entitled *The Lessons of History*, it observes, "When the group or a civilization declines, it is through no mystic limitations of a corporate life, but through the failure of its political or intellectual leaders to meet the challenges of change." The use of force against Nicaragua is a response to a quixotic call of the past. Rather than addressing issues of change, it attempts to negate change.

VI.
ISSUES
AND DILEMMAS

Third World Revolution and the Option
of Intervention

A small area in global terms, the size and population of Central America approximate those of the state of California. Although geographically close to the United States, in the minds of the American public it remains very remote. Yet, the present crises disturbing the region and Washington's response raise complex issues and dilemmas for the United States that go beyond the size and location of Central America. They stem largely from the willingness—or unwillingness—of Washington to tolerate change in the Third World. Behind that attitude lies the concern with security and authority. Many argue that Washington's determination to protect U.S. investments, trade, and loans abroad also shapes it.

The United States has intervened frequently in Mexico and the neighboring nations of Central America and the Caribbean, bombarding ports, blockading coasts, landing marines, maneuvering to overthrow governments, and occupying countries. Estimates of the number of these interventions during the course of the last century and a quarter vary, depending on who is counting and how they define intervention, but the base number exceeds 150. Nicaragua has felt the full weight of those interventions. No country has received more attention from Washington and the U.S. military, although Panama, Cuba, Haiti, the Dominican Republic, and Mexico certainly have garnered more than their share, too.

The purpose of the many interventions, consistent over a long period of time, was to ensure U.S. authority, control, and, hence, security in a region Washington always has deemed vital. In the process, U.S. businesses and banks enjoyed many preferences and plenty of protection as well. Its proximity to the United States, the strategic presence of the Panama Canal, and the sea lanes invite special military attention to the region.

Eventually anyone studying U.S. foreign relations must address the question of whether these numerous interventions have achieved their goal. Just what is it the United States has gained from these interventions? The answer is ambiguous. True, very importantly, the United States has maintained a powerful presence and control of the region. Threats, real or perceived, have been resolved in Washington's favor. Cuba provides a provoking exception. Or, rather than the exception, perhaps Cuba set in motion a new trend, the successful challenge to the United States, which has only begun to get underway. Obviously, the moral, financial, and physical costs of intervention rise geometrically as the century wanes. A doubt lingers as to whether they have provided long-term solutions to serious problems. If they had, then why at this late date, the end of the twentieth century, does the United States confront so many major crises there?

Furthermore, if U.S. interventions have been beneficial, why have they cost the Latin Americans so dearly in money, property, morale, development, and, most importantly, in human lives? It is estimated that more than 100,000 Guatemalans have been killed since 1954 under the military governments put in power by Washington. From the point of view of the Guatemalan Indians, a policy or, at any rate, the practice of genocide has been in effect for a third of the century. It is a modern holocaust, disguised as an anti-communist crusade, for which the United States must bear part of the responsibility. Morally, the interventions cast a grim shadow on the United

States, a shadow perhaps unperceived by the U.S. public but all too visible to Third World eyes. A political rationale can be applied: the interventions in Guatemala succeeded. No trace of "Communism" can be found; of course, for three decades neither was any manifestation of freedom or democracy visible. Furthermore, none of the Guatemalan governments since 1954 have enacted any basic reforms. In fact, they reversed the moderate agrarian reform of 1952. Guatemala basically retains the economic, political, and social structures inherited from the nineteenth century. Underdevelopment, dependency, and poverty are the threads woven into the economic fabric. For the overwhelming majority, the quality of life remains among the lowest in Latin America. Consequently, Guatemala is a social volcano ready to explode, that proverbial political time bomb waiting to go off. The presence of that potential instability cannot complement America's search for security. In that sense, the interventions have given the United States little peace of mind. Change of one kind or another has only been postponed; possibly that postponement may radicalize the form it eventually will take.

Nicaragua provides an even clearer example of the failure of intervention. In the case of Nicaragua, though, the United States actually occupied the country for more than two decades. If there was ever a moment for America to implant democracy and development, that seems to have been it. The United States controlled Nicaragua completely. Yet, the record disappoints even the most tolerant observer. Two decades of occupation weakened the economy, forged heavier chains of dependency, and inculcated none of the virtues of democracy. The Somozas constructed four decades of dictatorship on the U.S. intervention. The economist Jaime Biderman suggests that U.S. occupation might have "retarded the development of capitalism in Nicaraguan agriculture" and contributed to "the disintegration of the Nicaraguan economy."[1]

The journalist (and later historian) Carleton Beals judged the occupation as ruinous for Nicaragua, a political hug so tight from Washington that it nearly cut off the economic circulation of the client:

Nicaragua at the time of my visit [1928], after eighteen years of almost constant American meddling, much of which was attended by American financial, military and political control and by the employment of high-priced experts, was in a truly miserable condition. The argument for or against intervention cannot be based on its material benefits, actual or supposed, to a people; yet, it is significant that when I was there, its cities were dilapidated, its public buildings run down and dirty; that it had fewer miles of railway and roads than under Zelaya whom Knox, because of personal investments, overthrew in [sic] 1910; there are fewer schools. The north coast in Zelaya's time had over forty Government schools; today it hasn't half a dozen. The flourishing traffic of Zelaya's time up and down the great artery, the San Juan River and Lake Nicaragua, is today practically nonexistent. I later made the trip at the risk of my life. The post-office service, and in fact nearly every public service, was a joke. Nicaragua, under our paternal tutelage for so many years, had become the most back-ward and miserable of all Central American Republics.[2]

Furthermore, after reflecting on the sad state of Nicaragua in 1928, Carleton Beals concluded that the government the United States overthrew was superior to the ones Washington imposed on the country.[3] The physical intervention of the American military brought no advantages to the impoverished majority of the Nica-raguans, nor did the generous support the United States accorded the Somozas.

The economic misery of the majority was easily visible, statisti-cally measurable; difficult to measure would be the United States' lost opportunities for trade and investment which are more abun-dant with a developed nation than with an impoverished one. In that case, one has to question if the interventionist policies of Washington best served its own interests.

It is possible to speculate that constant meddling by the super-power — certainly when the interventions strengthen iniquitous in-stitutions inherent from the past — in conjunction with other his-torical factors can radicalize the search for change in the Third World. If, indeed, this theory holds some truth, then one can spec-ulate that the Reagan interventions in Central America, rather than resolving the crises, prevent reform and thereby promote revolution. When gradual change cannot occur, then sudden, violent, complete change probably will. It bides its time awaiting the propitious moment.

President Reagan, while obsessed with U.S. intervention in Central America, has demonstrated reluctance to promote it everywhere in the world, signifying that intervention is selective. After a tragic effort to intervene in Lebanon in 1983, the United States withdrew, its ardor cooled by the brutally bloody Middle Eastern response. Reagan's policy toward South Africa contrasts sharply with the one in Central America. Robert C. McFarlane, the president's national security affairs adviser, answering a question about South Africa on David Brinkley's show, stated, "The president believes it is not up to the United States to prescribe what is right for other people," a statement that should have gladdened the hearts of the Nicaraguans, except that what may be true for U.S. policy toward South Africa certainly does not apply to Central America.[4]

The president's comparisons of South Africa and Nicaragua have exposed an uninformed mind. Asked at a press conference on August 13, 1986, why he imposed sanctions on Nicaragua but refused to support them for South Africa, Mr. Reagan replied, "There is no comparison between South Africa and Nicaragua. In South Africa you're talking about a country, yes, we disagree, and find repugnant some of the practices of their government but they're not seeking to impose their government on other surrounding countries." He thus contrasted the South Africans with the Nicaraguans who "are intending to spread that revolution throughout Latin America." The president ignored—or was ignorant of—basic facts. South Africa, contrary to international law and mandate, occupied neighboring Namibia and intervened with impunity and violence in Angola, Mozambique, and other independent nations of southern Africa. No evidence of similar Nicaraguan intervention in Central America, let alone Latin America, exists.

The historic pattern of U.S. behavior in Central America in the twentieth century continues to favor the status quo, the preservation in broad terms of the institutions inherited from the nine-

teenth century bedecked as appropriate with the accoutrements
of the twentieth. Despite the heady rhetoric of President John F.
Kennedy in favor of democracy and development during the heyday of the Alliance for Progress, U.S. policy has remained consistent
and constant. Under the Alliance for Progress, U.S. military aid to
the Somozas rose sevenfold, while economic assistance doubled.
Following customary corridors, aid reached the rich who ignored
Kennedy's pleas for land and tax reforms. Predictably, the money
strengthened the grip of the elite on power and did nothing to
nudge reform forward. Basically, present policies follow this well-
worn path. The sobering reality by the end of the 1980s is that the
path does not lead to economic development and political stability.
Therefore, it cannot lead to the security the United States demands
in this hemisphere. In truth, it led precisely to the current crises
shaking Central America and disturbing the United States. Logic
dictates that more of the same policy will magnify, not resolve,
problems. *Time* editorialized, "Supporting the overthrow of a foreign government, even a detestable one, is a radical act that has
brought the U.S. to grief before. In the case of Nicaragua, it risks
prolonging civil war, justifying further internal repression by the
regime and heightening tensions all through the region."[5] In short,
elusive security becomes even more slippery.

For some, moral questions outweigh others. Given the evolution
of international society in the past five hundred years, the intellectual and moral trends counsel against the use of force, regarding it
as a violation of the sovereignty of states. Modern international
intercourse rests, at least theoretically, on the acceptance of the
legal equality of all states, and international law seeks to enforce
that juridical concept. Opposing the continuation of a policy of
intervention are cogent historical, moral, legal, and practical arguments. Sooner or later interventions engender security problems
for the United States. They create in the long run more problems
than they might solve in the short run.

Intensifying intervention in Central America isolates the United
States from all of Latin America. U.S. unwillingness to work with
the Latin Americans in solving the crises in a peaceful fashion now

reduces rather than augments the authority of the United States in the Western Hemisphere. On the broadest global screen, it pits the United States against the Third World and makes our allies increasingly nervous. Intervention may have been a viable policy for the powerful in the nineteenth century. It has been increasingly less so in the course of the twentieth, and it is hardly the policy with which to enter the twenty-first.

Terrorism

As terrorism pervades the world in the last half of the twentieth century, definitions of it multiply, many of them manipulated to serve the needs and interests of the speaker. The State Department favors this definition: "Terrorism is premeditated, politically motivated violence perpetrated against noncombatant targets by subnational groups or clandestine state agents, usually intended to influence an audience."[6] Brushing aside much of the nonsense written about terrorism, Christopher Hitchens hit the bull's eye with his remark, "The terrorist is always, and by defintion, the Other."[7] Accusations of terrorism can be a mirror reflecting and returning the finger pointed in blame.

Undeclared war and the covert activities entailed in it spawn violence of a nature associated with terrorism. To the extent that the violent actions against Nicaragua and Nicaraguans assume some of the characteristics of terrorism, the United States, largely through the CIA, has participated in or been a party to acts which many label as terrorist.

In no uncertain terms, President Reagan and members of his administration have condemned international terrorism. They preach an ideal of a world regulated by international law with respect for human rights, free from any taint of terrorism. They vehemently deny that the United States practices any form of terrorism. Yet, unfortunately, in the realities of international crises, the boundaries between legal actions/reactions and "terrorism" are often blurred or discerned differently in the eye of each beholder.

The Washington *Post* detected that confusion in the so-called

Hamlet speech in which Secretary of State George Shultz in late 1984 rationalized first-strike action against suspected terrorists. Furthermore, the newspaper linked U.S. succor of the contras to the support of terrorism:

Here we assert that he [Shultz] has simply not made the case that international terrorism is so immense and overwhelming a menace that it compels the United States to—in the name of the rule of law—take the law into its own hands on foreign soil.... Then there is the embarrassing question of what the United States is supporting in Nicaragua.[8]

A few months later, speaking before the War College, Shultz reemphasized that "international law" should not hamper active U.S. self-defense against terrorism.[9] He employed the "fight fire with fire" rationale. These statements reveal a vagueness in high government circles about the use of violence that raises moral problems or poses moral dilemmas.

Statements by CIA Director William Casey are not reassuring. After all, this man fingers the mechanisms to set off momentous actions and reactions that can be termed terrorist or counterterrorist, again depending on the eye of the beholder. Casey asserts, "We need not insist on absolute evidence that the targets were used solely to support terrorism. Nor should we need to prove beyond all reasonable doubt that a particular element or individual in that state is responsible for specific terrorist acts."[10] Our democratic beliefs proscribe this vagueness. Our courts routinely require juries to reach verdicts based on evidence proven beyond all reasonable doubt. Now, one of the most powerful men of the Reagan administration is able and certainly seems ready to trigger whatever mind-boggling destruction the CIA is capable of on assumptions, without absolute proof. Suspicion rather than proof provides ample terrain for mischief. To entertain these subversive thoughts as guidelines for U.S. policy or CIA action threatens our own future far more than an army of terrorists could.

Unfortunately, such thoughts already have been acted upon. They precipitated the disaster that could be forecast. In the covert actions of the CIA in Central America, no action has received more universal condemnation than the mining of three Nicaraguan harbors. The CIA laid the mines secretly; no one knew where they were; they exploded indiscriminately; the known victims were innocent Nicaraguan fishermen and crew members of foreign freighters, that is, noncombatants. In short, the action fits the State Department's definition of terrorism. Indeed, those CIA operations bore the stamp of terrorism to most observers. Even though Secretary of Defense Caspar Weinberger denied on April 9, 1984, that the United States had anything to do with the mining, the Senate voted the following day, eighty-four to twelve, to condemn U.S. participation in the mining incident. World opinion uniformly condemned the mining. There seemed little distinction between the secret mining of the Nicaraguan harbors and the earlier indiscriminate sowing of mines in the Red Sea that Washington had denounced and decried as terrorism. Furthermore, the Secretary of Defense blatantly lied to the press and to the American people. Was this his first and only falsehood in office? A moral issue emerges when a public official knowingly and willfully lies.

Nicaragua brought the United States before the World Court to stop the mining. The United States refused to go. The refusal further tarnished Washington's international image. Laurence H. Tribe, Professor of Constitutional Law at Harvard University, summarized much of the concern raised by the mining when he wrote:

President Reagan rightly invokes international law to denounce terrorism, but when other nations attempt to judge his foreign policy by the same set of rules, he prefers to pick up his marbles and go home. . . . Government under law is no mere game that we can quit whenever we don't like the rules. By stalking out of the World Court, the Reagan Administration derailed progress toward a world in which nations are governed by something other than the law of the jungle.[11]

The sudden exit from the Court further muddied murky legal waters and aroused suspicions of the depth of dubious activities in which the United States engaged in Central America. The subsequent revelation of a CIA-written manual for the contras advising "neutralization" of Nicaraguan officials only strengthened fears that at least a part of the U.S. governmental apparatus was involved in terrorist-tainted operations.

Those fears also arise from the use to which the contras put U.S.-supplied funds, training, and weapons. Associated in international opinion with Washington, those contras kill and wound far more civilians than military. In fact, they rarely engage the Nicaraguan army. One target of the contras is teachers; another, schools. In May 1980 they murdered a literacy teacher, and between then and August of 1985, 23 primary school teachers and 135 popular education teachers died at their hands. They destroyed 15 rural schools and forced 647 popular education centers to disband.[12] Doctors, nurses, medical workers, and lay leaders of Christian groups are other primary targets. An indiscriminate planting of land mines terrorizes the civilian population whose members become their indiscriminate victims.

While the questions of what is terrorism and who are the terrorists receive conflicting answers, generally with regard to Nicaragua both terrorism and terrorists are associated with the contras. Because of the direct link between Washington and the contras, the United States becomes associated directly or indirectly with terrorism. In the case of the mining of the ports the association is more direct than indirect. The implications raise serious moral issues.

The U.S. denunciations of global terrorism are less pursuasive than they might be because Washington supports the terrorist activities of the contras and, furthermore, cynically drapes them in the moral mantle of "freedom fighters." Washington may delude itself but not the rest of the world. Senator Howard Metzenbaum, Democrat from Ohio, did not let rhetoric beguile him. He judged, "Make no mistake, the contras are not freedom fighters. They are U.S.-backed terrorists."[13]

The international campaign to end terrorism would be well served by halting all aid to the contras and by returning to the jurisidiction of the World Court. After all, the rule of law is the most effective weapon to counter the rule of terror.

Morality and Foreign Policy

At the Nuremberg war criminal trials, Justice Robert Jackson of the United States Supreme Court stated with great assurance, "If certain acts and violations of treaties are crimes, they are crimes whether the U.S. does them or whether Germany does them. We are not prepared to lay down a rule of criminal conduct against others which we would not be willing to have invoked against us."[14] Those were bold words spoken with conviction, but Jackson was also saying the obvious: international law applies impartially to each and every nation. Forty years later, reasons exist to believe that the United States may have entered into treaties and under-taken international obligations which it is no longer prepared to honor. Difficult questions inevitably surface, and foremost among them would be the degree to which morality does guide the foreign relations of the United States. In short, will morality take prece-dence over expediency?

Thousands of screen Westerns for three-quarters of a century have depicted the morality tale of the triumph of the sheriff over the bad guys. The sheriff inevitably respected law and upheld order. Those Westerns, together with the other influences, have infused into American morality the conclusion that law breaking encour-ages lawlessness which, in turn, promotes disorder.

The overwhelming majority of Americans abide by the law. Cit-izens of every political stripe accept, celebrate, and encourage the rule of law. In few countries of the world do the judiciary systems enjoy the independence, power, and prestige they have in the United States. To the extent they have given it much thought, Americans probably accept as positive the concept of the rule of international law, orderliness on a global level. Given their predis-positions, they would consider reprehensible any flagrant breaking or flaunting of it. Certainly the fact must strike them as a supreme irony that the president they elected and revere as a "law and order man" stands in violation of treaties (laws of the land) and inter-national law. Image and reality diverge.

The question President Daniel Ortega brought before the UN

Security Council on July 29, 1986, summarized the choice between violence and law, between international order and anarchy. He emphasized the importance of the World Court decision for the peace, stability, and security of Central America and voiced Nicaragua's concern that the United States ignores the judgment in pursuit of military goals. On this particular issue, Ortega enjoyed widespread international support. In short, the issues do not exclusively resolve around relations between the American government and its former client but affect the most fundamental principles of international law. Latin America, like the rest of the Third World, relies on the rule of international law. When the United States behaves like might makes right, it condones violence, and the rest of the world becomes nervous.

The ramifications of the U.S. disregard for international law are extensive. One Nicaraguan official, Bayardo Arce, discerns these ancillary issues:

This represents a new stage in the history of Latin America. Not only has the U.S. declared war on a sovereign nation, they are also trying to buy the cooperation of other countries. The advisers will have to stay 20 kilometers away from our borders. Where are they going to put them? Have they asked permission of Costa Rica and Honduras for this?[15]

One point he makes is that by putting its military trainers in Honduras and/or Costa Rica and training contra forces there to invade Nicaragua, the United States obliges those two nations to break international law as well as all the treaties and charters of the UN and OAS proscribing intervention. Coercing small nations into lawlessness raises still other legal and moral questions. Nicaragua has filed action in the World Court to ban contra activity in Honduras and Costa Rica. It asks reparations from both neighbors. Obviously Nicaragua intends to keep the World Court busy, and in the process it acquires a new reputation as a champion of international law, a role that can only win it enthusiastic applause from the Third World, indeed from all those who place value on the rule of law. Ironically, the United States, once the knight protecting the delicate lady of international law, emerges in the 1980s as the villain sullying her, while a virtually unknown midget, Nicaragua, stands tall to protect her.

Escalating military activities violate international treaties, but they also counter U.S. law—the Neutrality Act, for one, which forbids aiding and abetting the overthrow of a foreign government from U.S. soil. A former Attorney General of the United States, Ramsey Clark, has made serious accusations against the Reagan administration's disregard for the rule of law. He charged:

Ronald Reagan has committed these acts in violation of international law, of the Constitution and of the laws of the United States. The President has no legal power to order U.S. forces to murder indiscriminately and terrorize those he styles his enemies. Such acts constitute high crimes and misdemeanors. Reagan's subversion of truth and the rule of law is the greatest threat facing the American people and indeed the world. We are responsible for our President's actions because we have the power to prevent them.[16]

These and similar charges raise serious moral questions about U.S. foreign policy and international behavior. When the United States marches to its own cadence in the international ranks, one must eventually ask who is out of step.

Of the many dilemmas raised by the war in Nicaragua, certainly foremost among them is how does a democratic country, an open society, conduct a secret campaign to overthrow a government with which it is officially at peace. Another unhappy precedent for the United States set by this war is that for the first time overt military aid flows from the U.S. treasury with the authorization of Congress and the consent of the president to a group seeking to overthrow a government with which the United States maintains diplomatic relations. After all, Managua and Washington exchange ambassadors. The United States has issued no official declaration of war. Yet, a war exists. The State Department, whose responsibility it is to maintain good relations with other friendly nations, finds itself in the bizarre position of pretending to maintain such relations with a nation with which another branch of the government, the CIA, carries on a war. Tellingly, the Defense Department, cognizant of the lessons learned in the Vietnam War—the impossibility of fighting a successful war in which the goals are poorly defined, for which there is little public support, and in which the allies are unsavory—wants as little to do with this war as possible. Perhaps the resolution of the dilemma emerges from commonsense morality. A powerful, basically moral nation like the United States has no business waging a covert war. It displays a lack of maturity and confidence unflattering to a superpower. Emotion has replaced rationality and thwarted a great nation from exercising its international responsibilities.

At the bottom line, the question confronting the United States after the June 27, 1986, decision of the World Court is whether the United States is for or against international law. While a negative response to the question does strengthen the policy of global unilateralism so characteristic of the Reagan years in the presidency, it negates—in actions if not in words—all previous efforts of the United States to strengthen international respect for law. A loss of U.S. international credibility results as nations comprehend the U.S. ambivalence toward its treaty obligations, its manner of willfully breaking them and painfully contorting language to justify and rationalize the action. Negating the Court's ruling launches an international voyage on the rough, uncharted seas of legal anarchy without the trusty compass of morality. Finally, the pragmatic and fundamental question must be asked: Is Nicaragua worth demeaning the international legal system? Priorities seem to be hopelessly confused.

The Domestic Impact of an Undeclared War

As the U.S. participation in its undeclared war in Nicaragua lengthens and intensifies, the repercussions within the United States grow, the contradictions become more obvious, and moral questions reverberate more intensely. The effects of war manifest themselves. The monetary cost of the war is an issue; the moral cost is too. In his unusually perceptive judgments of the United States near the mid–nineteenth century, Alexis de Tocqueville mused in *Democracy in America*, "No protracted war can fail to endanger the freedom of a democratic country. . . . All those who seek to destroy the liberties of a democratic nation ought to know that war is the surest and shortest means to accomplish it."

An interplay exists between international and national behavior. If one is immoral, the other will reflect it. History demonstrates the impossibility of compartmentalizing immorality. The techniques employed in secret wars abroad sooner or later show up at home. The desire to know what other governments and groups are up to melds into a similar urge to learn more about the opposition at home. The techniques of spying abroad become those for surveillance at home. Bribes to corrupt officials abroad take the form of subsidies at home to get more or less the same results. Watergate still looms as a reminder of the interplay, that chickens do indeed come home to roost.

The career of E. Howard Hunt illustrates that immorality recognizes no frontiers. He conspired under the auspices of the CIA to overthrow President Arbenz of Guatemala in 1954; he plotted with the CIA to invade Cuba at the Bay of Pigs in 1961; he supervised the Watergate break-in in Washington in 1972. Hunt saw no distinction between his international capers and his national intrigues. Sobering as the thought may be, Hunt probably was more the norm than the exception in his profession. He complained to the Senate Watergate Committee, "I cannot escape feeling that the country I have served for my entire life and which directed me to carry out the Watergate entry is punishing me for doing the very things it trained me to do." He carried that thought one step farther in an interview with *Time* (January 29, 1973): "You see, our Government trains people like myself to do these things and do them successfully. It becomes a way of life for a person like me."

It also became a way of life for a government. Illegality and immorality permeated it. The record of corruption and criminality boggles the mind. The Vice President of the United States, Spiro T. Agnew, resigned in 1973 under charges of taking bribes, evading income taxes, and general corruption. Meanwhile, in June 1972, the arrest of five men linked to the Committee to Re-elect the President and caught while they burglarized the Democratic party headquarters in Washington began a two-year drama that shook the American presidency to its foundations. Intensifying investigations into wrongdoing in the White House resulted in criminal charges against four of Nixon's cabinet officers and his two most important White House assistants. Scandals reached the top law enforcement officials: Attorney General Richard Kleindienst and L. Patrick Gray, acting director of the FBI, resigned. The CIA cast a murky shadow across these events. A former CIA agent, James W. McCord, was involved, as was Hunt and others of similar ilk. Thirty-eight high officials of the Nixon administration either pleaded guilty or were indicted for crimes. Finally on August 9, 1974, the President of the United States, Richard M. Nixon, resigned. American history offers no parallel to this lawlessness in high places.

Many of those men exposed in the Watergate scandals, like Hunt and Nixon, were deeply involved in foreign shenanigans that obviously had their domestic counterparts. Their case revealed that an intelligence mechanism constructed to subvert foreign governments could easily be directed to subvert national government. The great tragedy of U.S. political life, 1972–74, had some of its roots in the CIA interventions in Guatemala, Cuba, and Chile.

Within a decade after that tragedy, ominously comparable patterns appeared. The U.S. government refuses to abide by treaties, breaks international law, and denies the jurisdiction of the World Court. A disregard exists for national laws. Although the U.S. Constitution states that Congress shall declare war, the executive branch, once again, has involved the United States in a foreign war without consulting the legislature. The venerable Neutrality Act of 1794 made it a crime to initiate, organize, and/or provide money for military action against any foreign country with which the United States is at peace. The United States *officially* is at peace with Nicaragua. Nonetheless, the U.S. government, first the president and then Congress, initiates, organizes, and finances military action against Nicaragua. Private groups within the United States openly raise funds for the contras. Training camps for contras exist within the territorial limits of the United States.

In an effort to rein in an "imperial" president, Congress passed the Boland Amendment in 1982. It stated:

None of the funds provided in this act may be used by the Central Intelligence Agency or the Department of Defense to furnish military equipment, military training or other support for military activities, to any group or individual, not part of a country's armed forces, for the purpose of overthrowing the Government of Nicaragua or provoking a military exchange between Nicaragua and Honduras.

President Reagan found ways to circumvent the intent of the amendment. He continued to funnel money to the contras, all secretive, all illegal. The military maneuvers in Honduras provided an easy avenue to supply equipment, supplies, and funds. Faithful allies cooperated. Using "kickbacks" from arms sales to Saudi Arabia, money was secretly generated for the contras without congressional knowledge and so obviously without congressional approval and oversight. One intelligence source with extensive experience in Central America admitted to knowledge of "at least one major [arms] transaction" involving "$6 million to $10 million" of Saudi money used to purchase arms for the contras.[17] The Reagan administration also violated the Boland Amendment by assigning U.S. Marine Lieutenant Colonel Oliver North, a White House liaison to the National Security Council, without the knowledge or consent of Congress, to direct contra tactical operations, to act as a liaison for contra fundraising drives, and to orchestrate contra lobbying efforts on Capitol Hill. At any rate, as of June 25, 1986, Congress finally surrendered to executive importuning and gave the "imperial" president the approval he sought to wage his war.

In all of these shadowy dealings, the extent of CIA activity can only be surmised. The evidence suggests a lively reinvigoration of its role. Under William Casey, the CIA once again moves beyond mere gathering and evaluation of intelligence. In effect, certainly as far as Nicargua is concerned, it now makes and carries out foreign policy; and as its role expands, that of Congress contracts, particularly in regard to the making of U.S. policy for Central America.

The CIA keeps the contras fighting while at the same time using them to keep the funds flowing. Through the contras, the CIA lobbies Congress for special funding. Edgar Chamorro participated in the lobbying. According to him,

The CIA men didn't have much respect for Congress. They said we could change how representatives voted as long as we knew how to "sell" our case and place them in a position of looking soft on Communism. They suggested members whom we should lobby and gave us the names of big shots we should contact in their home districts.[18]

More than a little reciprocity emerges here: The U.S. intervenes in Nicaragua, while the contras intervene in Congress. A presidential executive order explicitly prohibits the CIA from such lobbying efforts. Like other laws, orders, and rules—the War Powers Act (1973), the Intelligence Oversight Act (1980), and an executive order of 1981 prohibiting the involvement of any U.S. agency in assassinations—it is honored in the breach.

The president's determination to overthrow the Nicaraguan government takes other tolls as well. The war divides American society, polarizing public opinion to a degree unknown since the Vietnam War. As the level of disinformation and misinformation from both the White House and the media mounts, the public becomes distrustful of both. Confidence in the intelligence community and the word of the president wanes. Public knowledge that the government is breaking national and international laws erodes its moral authority, while diminishing respect for the law. Government officials talk of "law and order" while their activities undermine both, encouraging public cynicism. A premium on military rather than legal or diplomatic solutions to international problems promotes violence and further contributes to disorder.

The public questions the expenditure of their taxes for dubious projects. The government answers evasively. The cost of the war is a manipulated statistic, once again truth being the victim of war. For public consumption, the cost of the war is a bargain. No true reckoning, however, has ever been presented the taxpayer since most of the expenditures for an undeclared war are secret, hidden, or disguised. Scholars, nonetheless, are making an effort to approximate the costs and publicize them. Their figures bear little relationship to those Washington announces. For 1985, Reagan officials announced that the United States spent $1.2 billion in Central America and the Caribbean. Scholars now estimate the real cost for U.S. policy in Central America in 1985 exceeded $9.5 billion (and some of the figures, including indirect expenses, go much higher than that). Their sum includes the money spent for security, military assistance, military exercises, military construction, and military forces.[19]

While the money directly spent in Central America amounted to 1 percent of the U.S. budget, it nearly equaled the combined total of the national budgets of the five Central American states. Many, including the Central American presidents, wonder whether the $9.5 billion might not be spent more wisely to invigorate the moribund Central American economies. In a region characterized by mass poverty, military expenditures are the ultimate luxury. Military hardware is economically nonproductive. Soldiers are nonproducers in the economy. Economies in need of investment and labor are deprived of both. The situation forecasts a bleak future in which it is hard to discern any beneficiaries except the generals.

Some within the United States resent the cuts in social spending at home in order to make war abroad. They suggest the money could be better spent on children's lunches, low-cost housing, and medical care for the aged. As the war lengthens, their complaints will multiply—as will the voices making them. Public perceptions of skewed priorities eventually will limit the war.

Opinion polls confirm that the public rejects the war. Jackson Browne captures the public anxiety in the lyrics to his popular song "Lives in the Balance":

> There's a shadow in the faces
> Of the men who fan the flames
> Of the wars that are fought in places
> Where we can't even say the names.

Browne's lyrics ask why the "men in the shadows … can be counted on to tell us who our enemies are?" Indeed, the American public will have increasing difficulty in figuring out why they are at war yet again in a Third World country.

In the meantime, unnecessary dilemmas confuse society. Moral questions bedevil the public. The major victims of the war are not always on the battlefield.

VII.

Charting the Future

The Contadora Peace Plan

Peace in Central America teeters on the question of whether or not Washington will accept the Nicaraguan revolution. On the one hand, the historical hostility of the United States toward New World revolutions and the flow of events since 1979 do not augur well. On the other, the world counsels peace; the Central American nations seek peace; and the public opinion polls clearly and consistently reveal the U.S. public wants peace. In the final analysis, of course, decisions made in Washington need not seek global or Central American approval and, at least in matters related to foreign policy, need not heed U.S. public opinion. Thus, according to its own inclinations, Washington will make the vital decision as to whether or not the isthmus will suffer continued war and devastation or enjoy peace and development.

The Reagan administration marches resolutely to war, although giving occasional but increasingly rare lip service to a peaceful resolution of the crises. Force, it has concluded, is the only way to rid Nicaragua of the Sandinistas. The logic is that without the Sandinistas, there will be no revolution; without the Nicaraguan revolution, the Central American crises will subside, perhaps disappear; without the revolution, Nicaragua will not challenge Washington and the United States will remain supreme and secure in Central America. Peace will reign.

Those ideas are simple but flawed. Peace imposed by foreign military boots deepens Central American resentment. In that resentment festers future discontent. The physical destruction of the Nicaraguan revolution, rather than close the door on crises, will open a Pandora's box of new ones. The Nicaraguan revolution is a manifestation of the Central American crises, not the cause of them. Peace will not return to Central America until the Central Americans address the basic problems of social and economic injustice. The crises spring from a desire, a need, to replace hoary institutions with new ones that will encourage economic development, not just permit periodic, cyclical economic growth. The economies of the Central American nations, each and every one of them, including Costa Rica's, are moribund. Overturning the Nicaraguan revolution will not breathe life into them. Under present conditions, increasing trade and aid will do little more than provide a momentary reprieve. To solve Central America's problems requires profound institutional change. The efforts to stifle the Nicaraguan revolution are nothing less than the quixotic compulsion to turn back the hands of time, the result, once again, of the politics of nostalgia.

The solution to the Central American crises lies not in returning to the past but in ferreting out from the past the roots of the crises in order to eradicate them. To do so requires a real, not an imposed, peace. No military solution exists. To the contrary, the military solution destroys and further impoverishes. It exacerbates the situation, thus deepening the crises rather than resolving them.

The Latin Americans understand the need for peace as the prelude to solving the complex problems of Central American economic development. They have put forth a plan, the Contadora Peace Plan, to reestablish peace in Central America. A war between the United States and one of the Latin American states pains all the Latin Americans. Another U.S. intervention, for whatever reason, offends their sense of nationalism. They understand that any war in Latin America destabilizes the entire hemisphere and indirectly threatens each nation. It undermines the precarious ground upon which the new democracies stand.

The foreign ministers of four nations with intense interests in the Caribbean and Central America—Venezuela, Colombia, Panama, and Mexico—gathered on the Panamanian resort island of Contadora on January 8–9, 1983, to initiate a diplomatic search for peaceful solutions to the mounting political crises in Central America. Their primary goal was to prevent a further deterioration of the relations between Nicaragua and the United States, to reconcile the United States to the revolution, and to address the anxieties of both Nicaragua and the United States about their national security. Their meeting constituted an effort to provide a Latin American solution, means whereby compromise and accommodation could be amicably worked out between Washington and the client. It signaled a major step in Latin American diplomacy, denoting its coming of age. No longer willing to wait for the traditional hemispheric leader to come up with a solution, the Latin American clients united to propose their own, to take fuller charge of their own destinies—another sign of changing times.

The task before the Contadora nations consumed more than a year and a half of sophisticated and delicate deliberations. On September 7, 1984, they presented their peace proposal. Basically, the twenty-one points of the proposal mandate the removal of all foreign military personnel from the region; border supervision to protect the sovereignty of each nation; democratic pluralism; and verification of compliance. The figures on pages 166–167 summarize the content.

Secretary of State George Shultz praised both the Contadora effort and document. Costa Rica, Honduras, El Salvador, and Guatemala indicated their conditional acceptance. Shultz congratulated the four on their adaptability before observing, "Nicaragua, on the other hand, has rejected key elements of the draft, including those dealing with binding obligations to internal democracy and to reductions in arms and troop levels."[1]

CONTADORA
Key Aspects of the Treaty

The parties—Costa Rica, El Salvador, Guatemala, Honduras, and Nicaragua—agree to:

Sec. 4, Para. 27
Withdraw Military Advisers

Timing: Within thirty days, a timetable for their "gradual withdrawal."

Allow Free Elections

Timing: Draw up election calendar on signing

Sec. 2. Para. 19
Bar All Arms Imports

Timing: Thirty days after signing

Let In Verification Commission

Timing: After signing, on demand of Commission of Verification and Control

Sec. 1 Para. 17
Bar All Foreign Military Exercises

Timing: Thirty days after signing

Sec. 5 Para. 29
Stop Arms Smuggling

Timing: After signing

Sec. 3. Para. 24
Close All Foreign Military Bases

Timing: Six months after signing

Sec. 6 Para 32
End Support For Guerrilla Movements

Timing: After signing

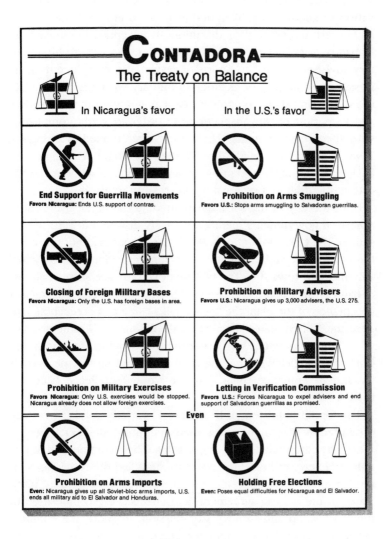

CONTADORA
The Treaty on Balance

In Nicaragua's favor | In the U.S.'s favor

End Support for Guerrilla Movements
Favors Nicaragua: Ends U.S. support of contras.

Prohibition on Arms Smuggling
Favors U.S.: Stops arms smuggling to Salvadoran guerrillas.

Closing of Foreign Military Bases
Favors Nicaragua: Only the U.S. has foreign bases in area.

Prohibition on Military Advisers
Favors U.S.: Nicaragua gives up 3,000 advisers, the U.S. 275.

Prohibition on Military Exercises
Favors Nicaragua: Only U.S. exercises would be stopped. Nicaragua already does not allow foreign exercises.

Letting in Verification Commission
Favors U.S.: Forces Nicaragua to expel advisers and end support of Salvadoran guerrillas as promised.

Even

Prohibition on Arms Imports
Even: Nicaragua gives up all Soviet-bloc arms imports, U.S. ends all military aid to El Salvador and Honduras.

Holding Free Elections
Even: Poses equal difficulties for Nicaragua and El Salvador.

The Secretary had misjudged. On September 21, 1984, Nicaragua accepted the Contadora Peace Proposal, the first Central American nation to announce publicly its decision to embrace the draft in its entirety and without modification. By accepting the document, Managua agreed to expel all Cuban, Soviet, and Eastern bloc military advisers, to halt all imports of armaments, to reduce its army in size, to scrap part of its stock of military weapons, to deny aid to Salvadoran rebels, to enter into a dialogue with the opposition, and to permit on-site inspections in order to verify compliance with these commitments. The acceptance stunned Washington. *Time* delicately reported, "The Sandinistas caught Washington off balance by abruptly accepting 'in its totality and without modification' the draft of a regional nonaggression treaty."[2]

Until the day of the Nicaraguan announcement, all five Central American governments seemed positively disposed toward the results of the Contadora efforts. President Reagan had not criticized the peace plan, and members of his administration seemed favorably inclined toward it. The elusive dove of peace seemed almost in hand. At that point, consternated by the unexpected Nicaraguan acceptance of the plan, the "peace talks came to a screeching halt after the United States signaled its displeasure."[3] Washington applied intense pressure on Guatemala, El Salvador, Honduras, and Costa Rica to delay signing the agreement, and during the delay it worked to convince them that the Contadora Peace Plan was flawed.

The foreign ministers of Honduras, El Salvador, and Costa Rica, prompted by Washington, presented a counterdraft on October 19, 1984, after their meeting in Tegucigalpa. Their draft permitted U.S. military exercises in Central America, modified the restrictions on foreign military advisers, omitted the protocol binding the United States to uphold the agreement, and changed the composition of the Verification and Control Commission. In short, the counterproposal maintained U.S. military might in the region, while requiring Nicaragua to reduce its defenses. Guatemala refused to sign it. Whatever merits the counterproposal may have contained, the realization that the United States, not Honduras, El Salvador, or

Costa Rica, directed the opposition to the Contadora Peace Plan, offset them. The heavy hand of Washington alienated world opinion which judged the process of turning an initially favorable response into negation as just one more piece of evidence of U.S. intervention and manipulation.

Meanwhile the Contadora Peace Plan of September 7 garnered international approval. The Inter-Parliamentary Union, over one thousand legislators representing one hundred countries, unanimously supported it on October 2, 1984. The UN General Assembly went on record on October 26 to endorse it.

The leak of a secret National Security Council document of October 30, 1984, authenticated just how heavy the pressure of Washington was on the Central American governments to reject the Contadora plan. It exalted:

We have effectively blocked Contadora group efforts to impose the second draft to the Revised Contadora Act. Following intensive U.S. consultations with El Salvador, Honduras, and Costa Rica, the Central Americans submitted a counterdraft to the Contadora states...[that] shifts concern within Contadora to a document broadly consistent with U.S. interests.... We have trumped the latest Nicaraguan/Mexican efforts to rush signature of an unsatisfactory Contadora agreement....Contadora spokesmen have become notably subdued recently on prospects for an early signing... although the situation remains fluid and requires careful management.[4]

President Reagan presided at that meeting. Without U.S. support, the Contadora plan could not move forward. Negotiations resumed and the war intensified.

Determined to find a satisfactory peaceful solution, the Contadora nations set to work again to negotiate the compromise required by U.S. opposition to the peace proposal. They enjoyed the friendly cooperation of the rest of the Latin American community. Even Chile's dour government rallied to the cause. In July 1985, the governments of Argentina, Brazil, Uruguay, and Peru announced the formation of the Contadora Support Group. Their foreign ministers met with their Contadora counterparts while all attended the inauguration of President Victor Paz Estenssoro in La Paz, Bolivia, in early August. Representatives of the eight Contadora and Support Group nations, democracies encompassing 85 percent of Latin America's population, then reconvened for two days in Cartagena, Colombia, on August 24, 1985. After endorsing the Contadora Peace Process, their Declaration of Cartagena cautioned, "If a peaceful and negotiated solution is not found for the Central American conflict, this will affect the political and social stability of all Latin America." President Belisario Betancur of Colombia summed up the goals of those attending the conference: "We consider it urgent to halt the arms race, to forbid foreign intervention in the area in all its manifestations and to prevent actions aimed at destabilizing the governments of the region." The participants realized that in the final analysis only economic development could ensure stability, but they also understood that no such development could take place so long as war ravages the region.

The Contadora group presented another treaty draft on September 12, 1985. It permitted the United States to keep its bases and conduct its military exercises in Honduras. The failure of the Central Americans to agree to the new proposal prompted the president of Venezuela to invite the Contadora and Support Group nations to Carabelleda in early January 1986 in order to find ways to break the impasse. They issued a document calling for the resumption of bilateral talks between the United States and Nicaragua; the end of foreign aid for the contras, "irregular forces," and insurrectional movements in the region; and resumption of the Contadora peace talks. Later that month at the inauguration of President Vinicio Cerezo in Guatemala City, the representatives of the five Central American governments signed a letter supporting the Carabelleda document and agreeing to resume talks.

At another level, pressure was being applied on Washington. On January 16, 1986, the eight ambassadors of the Contadora and Support Group nations called on Secretary of State Shultz to ask that the United States resume bilateral talks with Nicaragua. The Secretary turned down their request. On February 10, 1986, the foreign ministers of the same nations traveled to Washington to meet with Shultz and express their opposition to further aid to the contras. He listened with a deaf ear.

The Cartagena and Carabelleda declarations, as well as the pressures on Washington exerted by the eight governments that endorsed them, offered Washington an opportunity to withdraw militarily from Central America and avoid further intervention. Those actions would defuse the major crises of the isthmus and—if the concerns of the democratic nations are to be credited—a grave potential political crisis within all of Latin America. At the same time, the proposals promised Washington the security it demands: no Soviet or Cuban military presence on the isthmus. The Latin Americans will guarantee it. Cooperating with those eight nations would have given Washington a splendid opportunity to strengthen the democratic process of Latin America. The cold reception in Washington exposed the contradictions of the Reagan policy in Central America, causing Senator Patrick Leahy, Democrat from Vermont, to comment, "Our Government is in the strange situation of officially and piously endorsing the Contadora peace process, while simultaneously ignoring the pleas of the very countries who are looking for diplomatic settlement that would stop the fighting and defuse regional tensions."[5]

At their first summit meeting since the Nicaraguan revolution, the five presidents of Central America gathered in Esquipulas, Guatemala, at the invitation of President Cerezo to discuss the escalating crises. Whatever their disagreements—and they were many—the presidents concurred that the Contadora process offered the best political option for Central America to achieve peace and to reduce tensions.

Above all else, the Contadora Peace Process has been a Latin American effort to wrest Central America from the great power rivalries, to remove it from the East-West conflict, and to treat it within its Latin American context. The United States wants to see all Cuban, Soviet, and Eastern bloc influence removed from the region. It will not countenance those nations stationing troops, conducting military exercises, or building bases in Nicaragua or anywhere else in Central America. The Contadora Peace Plan would fulfill those goals. The catch, at least in the minds of Washington officials, is that the plan forbids *all* foreign military presence, a prohibition including the United States. It is very difficult for the United States to accept that limitation on itself—or, perhaps viewed differently, that exclusion of itself. Again, the basic security fears come into play. Washington is loath to limit itself militarily within the North American continent.

After nearly a century in the role as the major power of the region, the United States does not want to surrender power. It struggled during most of the nineteenth century to reduce Britain's sway over the region. The English-speaking, Protestant blacks inhabiting the Caribbean shores of Central America instantly remind even the most casual visitor of Britain's former presence. The victory over Spain in 1898; the Hay-Pauncefote Treaty of 1900 by which Great Britain formally exited from Central America, giving the United States a free hand there; and the Panama Canal Treaty of 1903 projected the United States forcefully into Central America. Washington now rejects the current efforts to restrict its action and authority. It negates a plan highly popular among Latin Americans without proposing to them an acceptable alternative. It does not acknowledge the reality that the conditions once complementing U.S. domination of Central America no longer exist. Latin America nationalism relentlessly challenges the patterns of imperialist domination established in the first decade of the century. To many—and particularly to many Central Americans and Latin Americans—the continued control of the United States is an anachronism, impermissible during the waning years of the twentieth century. The new realities that Latin America lives, and the old patterns that the United States prefers, collide.

The Reagan administration believes that any Contadora Peace Plan, if adopted, would strengthen the Sandinistas in power and thus contribute to institutionalizing the revolution. It also would limit U.S. military options in a region Washington considers vital to national interests and security. The reluctance of the administration to use the UN, the OAS, the World Court, or the Contadora process further testifies to its determined unilateralism in world affairs. Having identified Central America as a major security concern and a primary area within its sphere of influence, the Reagan administration refuses to collaborate with other nations to find a solution. Increasingly rare lip service and vacuous rhetoric are not sufficient.

A major obstacle to the Contadora Peace Plan is the contra conundrum. Nicaragua states that it will sign the treaty only after the United States terminates its support of the contras, while the United States responds that it will end its support only after Nicaragua signs the treaty. In this context, the Nicaraguans interpret the vote of the House of Representatives in June of 1986 in favor of Reagan's request of $100 million for the contras and the Senate concurrence on August 13 as congressional approval for U.S. intervention. The Contadora and support nations agree with that interpretation. A further complication for the Contadora process is Washington's refusal to sign any protocol to the plan obligating it to the treaty's provisions.

Other issues of disagreement revolve around arms reduction, foreign military maneuvers, and democratization. Nicaragua is willing to reduce the number of its offensive weapons but hesitates to cut back on defensive weapons so long as the threats of a contra invasion or a U.S. intervention exist. Nicaragua insists that U.S. military maneuvers stop, while the United States considers that such exercises are vital to contain the revolution and protect the other Central American countries from Nicaraguan "aggression." Costa Rica, Honduras, and El Salvador increasingly echo Washington's demand that the Nicaraguans democratize their government, opening it to the opposition and ensuring their fair participation. Nicaragua responds that it *is* a democracy in which a greater plurality of political views was expressed in the 1984 elections than was permitted—by practice if not by law—in the last presidential elections in El Salvador, Honduras, and Guatemala. Anyone who did not participate in the Nicaraguan elections, such as Arturo Cruz, voluntarily chose not to do so. It seems fair to conclude that more Nicaraguans are involved in grass-roots politics than at any time in the country's past, and equally true that Nicaragua has a more popular democracy—large numbers of people involved in and with the governing process and/or identifying with the governing process—than Guatemala, Honduras, and El Salvador, where the overwhelming majority is alienated from the political process. At any rate, the Nicaraguans believe that the democratization question is an internal one to be resolved by Nicaraguans, not outsiders, and to be resolved in a Nicaraguan way. Most Latin Americans agree that it involves matters of sovereignty that cannot be dictated from beyond the borders. Obviously any attempt by persons of one country to dictate norms of political behavior to those of another arouses howls of protest from the nationalists. They howl even more shrilly if the United States dictates those norms.

After more than three years of intensive efforts and hope, the "definitive date" for signing the Contadora Peace Plan, June 6, 1986, came and went. Instead of gathering signatures, the Contadora group produced a third peace treaty and issued the Panama Declaration. This treaty proscribed international military exercises and established the criteria to begin arms reduction, matters still hotly contended. The Panama Declaration speaks to the security concerns of both the United States and Nicaragua by requiring Washington to stop supporting the contras and Managua to maintain its nonalignment by abstaining from any political and military alliances. Nicaragua responded favorably to both the treaty and the declaration.

Prior to the congressional vote in mid-1986, the military defeat of the contras was a fact and the refinement of the Contadora Peace Plan an acknowledged accomplishment. That particular moment seemed propitious for the peaceful settlement of the crises, but into that historical moment intruded two conflicting events. The congressional approval of $100 million for the contras and the World Court decision declaring contra aid in violation of international law not only conflict but they also strengthen the resolve of both parties in the war.

In the course of many years of negotiations, hopes have risen frequently, only to be submerged in a sea of new frustrations. That the Contadora negotiations have navigated those stormy seas since

January of 1983 is a tribute to the considerable skills of the Latin American diplomats. They are determined to resolve the crisis of U.S.-Nicaraguan confrontation peacefully if it is at all possible. Very much on the positive side is the fact that thus far they have forestalled a U.S. invasion of Nicaragua.

Pax Latina

Unifying the region to pursue a project fundamental to Latin America's peaceful and democratic future, the Contadora Peace Process demonstrates the maturity of Latin American diplomacy. Latin Americans want to prevent the intervention of the United States and thereby prove to themselves that their sovereignty is more than a symbol. To them, the process declares Latin America's diplomatic independence, signifying the region's ability to cope with its own problems and come up with its own solutions.

Since 1983, nearly every Latin American political organization has voiced its support of the Contadora Peace Process. One of the most determined of those organizations, the Latin American Parliament—composed of delegates from the legislatures of the Latin American countries—issued a declaration at its meeting in Guatemala City on April 4–5, 1986, decrying the present isthmian crises as a threat to independence and democracy in Central America. It condemned intervention from the world powers in the region and emphasized the need for a Latin American solution:

The solution of these tensions and conflicts cannot be imposed from outside nor by recourse to brutal force. The solution must be Latin American, negotiated and pluralist. The principles sustained by the Latin American Parliament, which coincide with the efforts of the Contadora Group and the Lima Support Group, open the way to a Latin American solution that we are ratifying today. The Latin American Parliament ... defends the principles of self-determination, non-interference in internal affairs of other states, pluralist democracy, no foreign bases nor advisors and respect for human rights.[6]

The parliamentary declaration from Guatemala epitomizes the Latin

Americans' desire to resolve their own problems without the customary intervention of the United States, an intervention that the Latin Americans feel may benefit Washington in the short run but will be detrimental, as always, to Latin America.

While, on the one hand, if, in the words of President Betancur of Colombia, "very few actions in Latin America have stirred more interest and received the unanimous support of the international community than the Contadora Group's peace efforts," on the other, Washington continues to turn its back on those efforts. The determination of the Reagan administration to pursue a military solution—the historical U.S. response to change in Latin America—conflicts with the peace initiative put forward by the Latin Americans. Among other things, it pits the United States against its closest Latin American ally, Mexico. In the broadest perspective, it widens the distance between superpower and clients, forces the Latin Americans to hone their diplomatic skills, and strengthens the Latin American resolve to follow a more independent foreign policy.

The differing views actually highlight an old dichotomy dividing the hemisphere. At the time of another, much earlier, crisis, James Monroe believed the Western Hemisphere was a solitary unit in which the United States led, defended, and protected the rest—in short, playing the role of the dominant power. However, only one Latin American nation, Brazil, has ever acknowledged the Monroe Doctrine. The Spanish-speaking nations certainly never have. They subscribe to quite different ideas, those put forward by Simón Bolívar, a Venezuelan by birth but the Liberator of six Latin American nations stretching from Bolivia to Panama. Bolívar, a contemporary of Monroe, repeatedly stated that Latin Americans must act in union to protect their own interests which more often than not conflicted rather than coincided with those of the United States. Bolívar, like most Latin Americans, harbored contradictory feelings about the United States, attracted by some of its characteristics, repelled by others. At one point, he warned, "The United States appears by Providence to plague America with misery in the name of freedom."

Bolivarism has remained a firm ideal across time and throughout the vast region south of the United States. Generations of Latin Americans have paid homage to the ideas of the Liberator. Although inter-American in scope, those ideas touch nationalistic chords, for in confronting Washington nationalism widens to include regions and often all of Latin America rather than being confined to a solitary nation. Jealousies, isolation, and leaders who felt they had something to gain from allying with the United States consistently frustrated the realization of the Bolivarian ideal. Nonetheless, it has persisted for more than a century and a half to pervade thought and rhetoric and to inspire lofty hopes.

The Contadora process encapsulates the Bolivarian ideal. Furthermore, the process persists because the historical moment complements its pursuit. Its resurgence parallels a notable return to democracy in the hemisphere and the appearance on the political stage of a remarkable group of civilian leaders: Raúl Alfonsín of Argentina, Julio Sanguinetti of Uruguay, José Sarney of Brazil, Jaime Lusinchi of Venezuela, Alan García of Peru, Belisario Betancur of Colombia, Oscar Arias of Costa Rica, Vinicio Cerezo of Guatemala, and Miguel de la Madrid of Mexico. No region of the world of comparable size boasts so many extraordinary democrats in power at a given moment. Latin America never has before. These are exactly the types of leaders the United States should be working with, supporting them rather than ignoring them. Their allegiance to the Bolivarian ideal is doubtless strengthened by a reaction to the military governments which preceded most of them. Directly or indirectly the generals associated with Washington, and formally or informally they acquiesced in Monroeism. One of the foreign ministers of the military governments of Brazil, Juracy Magalhães, stated candidly in the mid-1960s, "What is good for the United States is good for Brazil," the kind of statement that enrages nationalists. The reemergence of Latin American democracy also coincided with the intensifying confrontation between Nicaragua and the United States. These two historical events converge to reinvigorate the Bolivarian vision of the Latin American community.

The Contadora Peace Process may be the most visible and dramatic manifestation of resurgent Bolivarism, but it is not the only one. Treatment of Cuba is another example. The United States pressured the Latin American governments in the early 1960s to break diplomatic relations with Havana and isolate the Cubans. All except Mexico did. In 1964, again at the insistence of Washington, the Organization of American States voted to suspend Cuba's membership. Largely ostracized from the Latin American community until the late 1970s, the reintegration of Cuba then occurred at an accelerating pace as military dictatorships fell and democracy returned. One by one the Latin American nations restored diplomatic relations with the island nation. In June 1986, Brazil, after a twenty-two-year break, dispatched an ambassador to Havana, one of the last of the Latin American nations to reopen relations. In September, the Cubans initiated a bimonthly shipping service to Brazil. At the same time, the Latin Americans accepted Cuba as an observer in the Latin American Integration Association, an organization hoping to form a common market. The United States is neither a member nor an observer. The Latin Americans embrace Cuba, whatever its government, as a part of their community with the indissoluble ties of culture, language, and history.

The contrast between the treatment the Latin Americans accorded Cuba in the 1960s and 1980s further accentuates their changing relationships with Washington: Latin America is asserting greater independence in its international behavior. Cuba's Deputy Foreign Minister Ricardo Alarcón correctly observed, "It is clear that an objective of the Reagan Administration was to reinforce the isolation of Cuba. Despite that being the declared policy, they are now unable to impose it." With regard to Cuba, the Latin American governments clearly manifest their greater independence of action. Alarcón stated that Cuba had no desire to rejoin the OAS because of the long history of U.S. domination of that organization. He summarized the Bolivarian view in his observation: "With the United States, there can be dialogue, communication, but the United States does not belong to this region."[7]

Gigantic Brazil, the world's sixth-largest nation and eighth most populous, boasts the world's tenth largest economy and increasingly constitutes a major challenge to U.S. domination of the hemisphere. Impressive economic growth during the twentieth century propels Brazil's need for an independent foreign policy in which the search for markets supersedes ideological considerations. Certainly in this case, practical matters chart a foreign policy detaching Brazil from the Pax Americana. Philosophically, Brazil has accepted the same ideals that Bolívar expressed.

Most global forums in the 1980s find Brazil opposing the United States. Critical of U.S. support for the rebels fighting the government of Angola, Brazil maintains close relations with Luanda and exports impressive quantities of goods to the Angolans. Africa in general offers Brazilian industry an important market. Brazil provides credit to and technicians for Managua. It belongs to the Contadora Support Group. In a major step toward economic development, Brazil and Argentina, with a combined population of 165 million, agreed in 1986 to an economic integration plan to replace billions of dollars of imports with local products, a vital step toward the economic development of both nations. Brazil definitely has its own diplomatic agenda both within and without the hemisphere, and it is quite independent from that of the former hemispheric leader. Its size, population, and economic vitality suggest its leadership within Latin America will grow as that of the United States declines.

As Latin America withdraws from the Pax Americana, so does Europe. At the same time and not coincidentally, these two large and important regions are rediscovering each other. The Central American crises accelerate that trend. The Europeans listen sympathetically to the cries of injustice from Central America. Generally they condemn the war against Nicaragua. Their conclusions and recommendations obviously differ from those of Washington. This time, instead of passively observing, they lend their support to the Contadora Peace Process, uniting with the Latin Americans in opposition to the United States. Future implications of this new coupling have not yet concerned Washington.

The Contadora Peace Process, highlighted by the declarations of

Cartagena, Carabelleda, and Panama, signal a turning point in Latin American diplomacy, a new confidence, a new reality which heralds a Pax Latina within their part of the hemisphere. Clearly the democratic governments exert more independence in their diplomacy than their military predecessors did. Their independence should be seen positively now that Washington makes a great fetish of advocating pluralism in Latin America.

In contrast to Washington, the Latin Americans do not interpret the Central American crises as a part of the East-West conflict. Rather, they understand that they spring from underdevelopment and confrontation with the United States. Nonetheless, the crises alarm the Latin American democracies, albeit for quite different reasons. The intensifying warfare, militarization, and foreign interventions threaten the democratic future of all of Latin America. A U.S. invasion of Nicaragua has the potential of sparking a political explosion throughout Latin America. The Declaration of Cartagena bluntly warns, "If a peaceful and negotiated solution is not found for the Central American conflict, this will affect the political and social stability of all Latin America."

At no time in the twentieth century has U.S. leadership in the Americas been less effective or more seriously challenged. The determination of the Latin Americans to find and put forward their own solutions not only confirms the demise of the Pax Americana but lends credence to the belief in the emergence of a Pax Latina. Such a Pax Latina, nurtured by the powerful forces of nationalism and Bolivarism, promises the Latin Americans greater control of their own destinies.

The United States and the Third World in the Twenty-first Century

Obsession replaces realpolitik in the foreign policy of the Reagan administration toward Nicaragua. The outcome is predictable. It blurs Washington's vision of the hemisphere. Vast, volatile Latin America shrinks to a subsidiary position as a small isthmian nation looms larger than life. Officials see less clearly those problems—

debt, trade deficits, economic recession, social ferment—that threaten the stability of major nations and focus not at all on the declining leadership of the United States in Latin America. A Pax Latina begins to replace the Pax Americana without Washington being aware of the shift, let alone the consequences.

Obsession obliterates perspective. No effort is made to understand other peoples on their own terms. Powerful political and emotional forces such as nationalism are ignored or, through ignorance, challenged. A foreign policy clouded by obsession takes little heed of rational priorities. To "win back" Nicaragua, Washington is willing to alienate Latin America. To reexert its authority over Managua, it is willing to diminish its influence in Mexico City, Caracas, Bogotá, Brasília, and Buenos Aires.

One of the many realities to which obsession blinds Washington is that Nicaragua wants—and needs—correct relations with the United States. Nicaragua wants military hardware from the United States, loans from the U.S. government and banks, trade with North American markets, investments from U.S. capitalists. In each and every instance, the Reagan administration has prohibited the intercourse because it ideologically dislikes the FSLN and the revolution; even before his election as president, Ronald Reagan perceived Nicaragua as a "client state" of the USSR. Of course, necessity—shaped in large part by U.S. behavior—in time may change perception into reality, and, if so, Washington will have done more than its part to bring about the transformation. Obsession has become so blinding that it turns into disasters situations which a diplomacy of realpolitik could forge into advantages.

At the very worst, Nicaragua should be no more than an irritant to U.S. diplomacy. To make it one of the centerpieces suggests that Washington has lost its sense of proportion. Only the CIA and the contras benefit from the policy of confrontation, a reality sensed if not perfectly comprehended by the public which disapproves of Reagan's Central American policy. Public opinion polls on the Nicaraguan issues, since the first one in 1981, consistently and overwhelmingly reject his policy. For example, the Washington *Post*–ABC poll released on June 25, 1986, showed that 62 percent opposed any aid to the contras, while 29 percent favored it. The public correctly equates expensive adventures abroad with cuts in social programs at home. U.S. banks, businesses, and investors lament the loss of one more market, small as it may be.

Reagan's aggression against Nicaragua isolates the United States internationally. Its leadership role in Latin America has declined to its lowest level in the twentieth century. The new clients, the contras, are an international pariah. Their support depends exclusively on the United States, but they can never serve the best interests of their generous sponsor.

Those interests can best be served by an economically developed Central America. Only that development will provide the political stability upon which the genuine security of the United States can rest. Military operations engender economic destruction, not development.

Any foreign policy for Central America—or the Third World, for that matter—that does not have as its primary concern economic development does not honestly address the needs and desires of the United States for security. Ironically, while the Reagan administration makes a great fetish of national security, spending record amounts of money on defense, it undermines the stability of Central America through its heavy emphasis on military solutions. The most recent plan to pour $53 million in equipment and training into the police forces of Guatemala, El Salvador, Honduras, and Costa Rica is undertaken in the mistaken belief that order and stability can be established by more and better-trained police. It is worse than money down the drain. The need for more police signifies social instability, but the increase in the police forces does nothing to alleviate the causes of that instability. In fact, over the long run, one might even argue that it will increase it. Order and stability will characterize Central America only when there is a higher degree of social justice brought about by economic development. The $53 million would be far more wisely invested in land reform which would truly contribute to reduce the causes of instability.

No historical basis exists for the faith in the ability of the Central American military to provide the United States with the security it seeks. A consistent record of venality and violence characterizes the Central American military. To speak of it as a contributor to development and democracy assigns to both of those concepts a meaning that, while it might show Orwellian imagination, distorts them beyond recognition. The current examples of CIA and contra "payoffs" to the Honduran military and of Salvadoran officers selling arms to the rebels suggest the long history of greed and corruption which extensive U.S. military training has done little or nothing to eradicate. By the inherent nature of its structure, the military can contribute nothing to the nurturing of democracy.

Few, except Reagan officials, conclude that a military solution can resolve those abysmal social and economic conditions that spawned revolution in Nicaragua and threaten to do so elsewhere. Interestingly enough, even the Pentagon harbors serious reservations about marching into Managua. General Wallace H. Nutting judges the talk of invading Nicaragua as "counterproductive." With an unusual historical insight, he concludes, "We are paying a high price now for what they [the Nicaraguans] call military intervention for 50 years. I don't think we want to do that again. ... I think we are going to have to learn to live with Nicaragua."[8] If U.S. interventions in Cuba, Haiti, the Dominican Republic, and Nicaragua, to mention only the most frequent and longest ones, consistently failed to implant democracy and development, upon what basis can one expect yet another intervention to reverse the well-established and documented record of failure? Apparently the general's recommendations—even though the Joint Chiefs of Staff echo them—carry little weight in the White House, where officials spurn Pax to court Mars. Concerning crises in a more distant part of the world, President Reagan once remarked, "This return to violence is abhorrent—all the more so because it is so useless. ... There is no military option for solving the difficult conflicts of the Middle East."[9] Alas, his obsession with Nicaragua prevents him from applying his own wisdom to the crises of Central America. The obsession with planting the seeds of democracy in the arid military garden of Central America represents more than folly; it indicates that the gardener has no desire for them to sprout.

In an unusually philosophical mood, Secretary of State George P. Shultz observed, "History will not do our work for us."[10] Indeed, people must actively sculpt their own history, but the task is infinitely simpler when people use as tools the major forces at work during a given historical time period. Mr. Shultz's major link with history is that he wants to repeat it, to return to an era when differences with the small Central American nations could be resolved by dispatching half a dozen gunboats and a few hundred marines. Putting aside the specious case of Grenada—where, in any case, an awesome flotilla of warships, an air force, and an army were dispatched—that era is over. To try to repeat that particular aspect of the past in the 1980s will detonate disaster. If Washington is to ally itself with the force of history, the thrust toward change rather than the preservation of the past would serve it better. Central America, Latin America, and the Third World are changing; U.S. policy toward them remains static. The war with Nicaragua suggests in microcosm the problems awaiting the United States as it clings to policies of the past in its relations with the Third World. Clearly these policies no longer speak to the realities of the late twentieth century. They indicate that Washington is unprepared to enter the twenty-first.

Fiery debates consume the controversial topic of the Nicaraguan revolution and the proper U.S. reaction to it. From the ashes a proper foreign policy may yet arise. Most discussion seems to center on whether Moscow or Washington should shoulder the blame for the crises. Indications are that the debate also smolders—if it does not rage—within the confines of the closed chambers of the administration. The Pentagon may well be the least enthusiastic participant in the war. Failure to detect a national consensus favoring the war disturbs the officers. One army colonel muses, "The problems down there are not military, they are political and economic. You shouldn't send soldiers to solve political and economic problems." Another advises, "Mr. President, don't send us to war unless you have clear-cut political goals and attainable military objectives."[11]

Other evidence of disagreement surfaces when State Department purges occur as ambassadors such as Robert White, Lawrence Pez-zullo, and John Ferch—as well as the chief of the U.S. Interest Section in Havana, Wayne Smith—exit, not without firing off a volley of criticism at U.S. policy. One conclusion is absolutely clear: the State Department does not make the policy for Nicaragua. It comes directly out of the White House.

At one point, the president asked Henry Kissinger to recommend an appropriate policy. His National Bipartisan Commission on Central America reported in January 1984, serving up a warmed-over soufflé of formerly unpalatable policies. Strongly influenced by the Alliance for Progress, it recognized social injustice in the isthmus but conluded that the Soviet Union and Cuba manipulated the genuine desires for change. It recommended both economic and military aid. Dust settled on the report. Neither the president nor anyone else, for that matter, refers to it any longer. The White House unflaggingly follows its policy of nostalgia, ignoring reality, violating history, and separating knowledge from action.

Some applaud the president, urging him to repeat the past. The Cuban American National Foundation publishes pamphlets that unequivocally brand Nicaragua communistic—"Nicaragua is a country ruled by Communists, and solely Communists, whose unanimous and unswerving goal is to turn it into a totalitarian state"—and advocates military removal of the Sandinistas.[12] Among the "think tanks" complementary to the Reagan administration, the American Enterprise Institute supports "democratic developmentalism," which sounds promising but turns out to be hopelessly vague. While it counsels a diminished U.S. presence and greater restraint, it also advocates continuing, perhaps even expanding, military and economic assistance. It believes that more trade, along with the aid, will ease Central America's crises without any acknowledgment that old trade and aid patterns may have contributed to the crises.[13] At any rate, the "aid and trade" formula, an old Washington standby, echoes the recommendations of the Kissinger report, or could it be vice versa?

Another range of private groups, exemplified by the Inter-American Dialogue, the International Peace Academy, and the Institute

for Policy Studies, supports policies that terminate aid to the contras and implement the Contadora Peace Process. While these
groups speak admirably to the immediate crises, they address
longer range policy problems less decisively. These groups find
some strong allies within Congress, such as Patrick Leahy in the
Senate and Michael D. Barnes, Chair, Subcommittee on Western
Hemisphere Affairs, in the House of Representatives. While critics
of Reagan's behavior in Central America are by no means mono-
lithic in their statements, they seem to agree that the present policy
of nostalgia does not serve America's best interests.

In formulating a policy toward Nicaragua, the first and foremost
concern is national security. The United States does not want and
will not tolerate Soviet bases of any kind in Nicaragua, nor for that
matter any Cuban bases. Quite frankly, neither will Nicaragua. Although you would not know it by listening to the rhetoric from
Washington, Nicaragua and the United States agree: no foreign
bases in Nicaragua or in Central America. Nicaraguan Ambassador
to the United States Carlos Tunnermann put it succinctly: "We will
allow no Soviet or American bases. We have said this repeatedly."[14]
Minister of the Interior Tomás Borge has affirmed frequently that
there will "never be any foreign military bases here."[15] Publicly
President Ortega and Vice President Ramírez emphasize those assurances. Ortega expressed a willingness to address the major concern of Washington: "If the United States feels that Nicaragua is a
threat in the region, we will look for mechanisms of security so
the United States feels secure."[16] Speaking directly to the fears
Washington harbors of a Soviet military presence, he assured,
"There is no Soviet military base in Nicaragua. There are no Soviet
troops. We don't have military maneuvers with the Soviets, and we
are willing to put all of those facts in a treaty with the United
States."[17] Appearing before the UN Security Council, the president
of Nicaragua appealed, "We must repeat that we do not want confrontation, that we have not come to the Security Council to launch
insults against the North American government, but to seek peace
and respect for international law."[18] These statements sound reas-

suring and reasonable to most of the world. Thus far, Reagan officials routinely classify them as "propaganda ploys."

The United States need not act solely on the "reassuring" words
of Daniel Ortega. If signed, the Contadora Peace Treaty would forbid foreign bases as well as any foreign military presence in Central
America. If that treaty is not sufficient, then Nicaragua stands ready
and willing to sign a treaty with the United States in which it
declares the inadmissibility of foreign bases in return for U.S. guar-
antees of non-intervention directly or through the contras. In short,
Managua wants to accommodate the genuine security concerns of
the United States if Washington will do the same for Nicaragua.
The matter could be resolved easily, and should Nicaragua for
whatever reason break the treaty, then the United States would be
justified to take whatever action necessary to guarantee its own
security.

As previously stated, the Contadora Peace Plan is capable of satisfactorily defusing the present crises. Adopting the plan will require compromise from both Managua and Washington, but compromise lubricates diplomacy. Compromise and accommodation
have been the norm of peaceful international behavior.

Global unilateralism, however, avoids those norms. As the intervention in Grenada and the bombing of Libya illustrated, quick,
media-oriented action replaces diplomacy. Washington hopes that
some similar unilateral action may yet rid Nicaragua of the Sandinistas but dithers, understandably cautious about the consequences, yet reluctant to move in the other direction and accept
the Contadora treaty.

The reason for the reluctance arises basically from the desire to
retain a military presence within Central America. One can rationalize and understand that desire, particularly as it springs from
historical habits. However, the twenty-first century will require
new habits. Few, if any, of the Third World nations will want to
host the armies of the superpowers. A major characteristic of the
last half of the twentieth century has been the political emergence
of the Third World. Major characteristics of the dawn of the new
century will be its political vitality, economic development, and

cultural individuality. The current behavior of the United States in Central America—and one could add other regions of the world—indicates it must prepare for this transition. Even the richest and most powerful nation cannot stem the tides of change forever.

While the United States has achieved a remarkable civilization for itself within its own unique geographical and historical milieu, it offers few economic, political, or social solutions that can be successfully grafted onto other cultures. Latin Americans are perfectly capable of understanding and, if left alone, of solving their own problems. The historical truth is that they have had precious few opportunities to try during the last half a millennium. Always thought-provoking is the realization that under the Incas, the Indians of South America ate better and enjoyed more justice than at any time since the conquest. The arrival of the Europeans and further exposure to the cultures of the North Atlantic plunged the population of the former Incan Empire into a degradation from which they have yet to recover. The possible lesson to be extracted in the late twentieth century from that reality is the ability of people left alone to solve their own problems more satisfactorily than outsiders can.

Leaving Latin America alone does not mean it will exist in a vacuum. It means that Latin Americans will make decisions for themselves and that Washington will respect those decisions. The reality of distance gives Moscow little choice but to do likewise. An affinity—more acquired than natural—attracts Latin Americans to the United States. Trade will continue, and, as Latin America develops, it should increase. In most cases, respect rather than regimentation from Washington will bring into play good relations and cooperation.

Any successful future foreign policy for Central America—and by extension for the Third World—will require from the world's premier power forbearance and patience and an effort to understand other peoples on their own terms: how they see themselves and what they want. In short, it requires diplomacy and not the marines.

What the United States can probably expect in Central America as larger numbers of people become politicized is a desire on their part to better utilize their human and natural resources for the benefit of, if not everyone, then for the largest number possible. The overwhelming cry of the dispossessed majority is for justice, an end to iniquitous institutions whose burden they bear but whose benefits elude them.

Any government responding to that cry will first address the fundamental question of agrarian justice. The devolution of unused and underused lands to the landless who want to work them is a primary necessity in societies that produce abundantly for export but niggardly for national consumption, requiring the importation of basic foods. In that economic pattern, hard currencies that should be used to promote development buy the foods the country is perfectly capable of producing in abundance.

An agrarian reform will create a new peasant class. To be effective producers, these peasants must have access to credit, fertilizers, seeds, and technical assistance. Their productivity would raise the low level of nutrition for the majority, and they could also contribute to an increase of exports. A strong, healthy peasant class is essential for economic prosperity and political stability. The agrarian reform will not take place without howls of protest and probably some physical resistance from landowners. Resolving the resultant conflicts is the business exclusively of the Latin Americans.

The tax burden should rest squarely upon those who derive the most benefits from society rather than, as at present, on those who already bear the heavy burdens of poverty. Indirect taxation, a major source of revenue in most of the republics, falls heaviest on the poor. Again, the privileged will protest and out of habit appeal to Washington to eliminate the "communists." Washington must realize that matters of internal taxation in Latin America, like those of agrarian reform, are none of its business.

The small size of each of these five Central American states suggests that they can gain economic strength through complementary trade relations. Encouragement of the revitalization of the Central American Common Market will expand their trading opportunities.

Ready access to that expanded market should strengthen industrialization, but Central America's industrialization to be meaningful must reflect local realities. It must serve local needs. First and
foremost, it should be labor-intensive to provide jobs for the le-
gions of unemployed and underemployed. Also, it must produce
basic necessities for larger numbers of the population, shifting away
from a growing concentration on assembly plants for consumer
items for the North American market.

Monies diverted from sterile militarism should flow into badly
needed public works projects. Central America desperately needs
hospitals, clinics, schools, vocational training centers, and low-in-
come housing. Public works projects will supply the basic needs
of the impoverished majority, while at the same time creating jobs.

For too long and with obviously unsatisfactory results, the Central American nations have followed an outwardly oriented development policy emphasizing industrialization through exports,
agrarian exports, foreign investments, and low wages to make industrial and agrarian goods internationally competitive. The policy
fostered a dependency on foreign markets and investments without
generating national development. Gradually, attention is now shifting to a more inwardly oriented plan for development that stresses
food self-sufficiency and the encouragement of local small industries that produce for the home market. Its advocates insist that
this basic step, usually leaped over in the rush to export and earn
hard currencies to buy luxuries, cannot be omitted in the pursuit
of development. They may be correct. They deserve a hearing. At
any rate, the twentieth century has demonstrated that developed
nations seldom are able to solve the problems of underdeveloped
nations. In truth, they have probably exacerbated them. The solutions must arise from within, from those who know local
strengths and weaknesses, potentials, desires, and cultural affinities.
Foreign theories have only provided the Central Americans with
myriad rainbows whose pots of gold proved to be illusory. For its
own ultimate benefit, the United States must draw the obvious
lesson from past experience that no investments or loans are pref-

erable to the dictation, direct or indirect, of how the money will be spent.

If the United States wishes to use its energy, wealth, and goodwill to help to promote the changes that most Central Americans will undertake once left alone, then it might passively contribute to the expansion of the reforms. The United States could help to fund the reforms initiated by the Central Americans themselves by diverting dollars from military expenditures. Washington probably will discover that once left alone to resolve their own problems and once change, whether by reform or revolution, is underway, civil war and guerrilla activity will decline and then disappear. The very changes enacted will undercut any influence that Cuba or the Soviet Union might exert.

Complexities will arise as they must in changing societies. Stress and tension will appear, hopefully only short-term characteristics. Some transitory injustices will occur in lands long marked by massive injustices. Once genuine development—the use of the nation's resources for the greatest good of the greatest number, to paraphrase Jeremy Bentham—is underway, political stability will follow. That political stability will ensure the security the United States seeks and demands. Furthermore, as economic development advances, then markets expand and the trade between the United States and Central America will interlock more naturally to the greater benefit of both. After all, the United States is more likely to do a booming business with developed rather than underdeveloped nations. In the intermediate to long run, change, as chaotic as its initiation may be, ensures better and more satisfactory relations between Central America and the United States. Central America then will have ceased to be the horror story in U.S. relations with the Third World and may well serve as a model.

To initiate a resolution to the present U.S.-Nicaraguan conflict, Congress must play an aggressive and positive role. The House of Representatives should be expected to reflect the will of the American people. Their will has been expressed repeatedly through public opinion polls. They reject U.S. intervention. They reject the contras. No popular will exists for war against Nicaragua. Even the most popular president in recent memory cannot sway public opinion to favor it. On this issue, Congress should pick up the fallen mantle of leadership. To do so, Congress must now reverse itself to reaffirm the U.S. commitment to non-intervention and the peaceful solution of international problems by definitively terminating all aid to the contras and endorsing the Contadora Peace Plan. National security will be thrice served. Friction with our global allies over Nicaragua would end, our leadership in Latin America could be restored, and a peaceful Central America, free of entangling alliances, could invest its energies into economic development, the prerequisite for political stability.

SOURCE NOTES

Chapter I. Obsessed with Nicaragua

1. Los Angeles *Times,* February 23, 1985.
2. *Envio,* 5:55 (January–February 1986): 5.
3. Jaime Biderman, "The Development of Capitalism in Nicaragua: A Political Economic History," *Latin American Perspectives* 36 (Winter 1983): 20.
4. Bruce Marcus, ed., *Nicaragua: The Sandinista People's Revolution* (New York: Pathfinder, 1985), p. 174.
5. Tony Jenkins, *Policy Focus,* no. 3 (Overseas Development Council, 1986), p. 8.
6. *In These Times,* March 13–19, 1985.
7. *Times of the Americas,* June 25, 1986.
8. *Envio,* 5:55 (January–February 1986): 31–32.
9. *Congressional Record,* March 27, 1986.
10. Los Angeles *Times,* March 10, 1985.
11. Melvyn P. Leffler, "The American Conception of National Security and the Beginnings of the Cold War, 1945–1948," *American Historical Review* 89:2 (April 1984): 354.
12. *Christianity and Crisis,* February 17, 1986, p. 42.
13. Thomas Etzold and John Lewis Gaddis, *Containment* (New York: Columbia University Press, 1978), pp. 226 and 227.
14. Los Angeles *Times,* April 23, 1983.
15. Los Angeles *Times,* August 7, 1985.
16. Los Angeles *Times,* March 3, 1985.

17. *Nation,* April 19, 1986, p. 542.
18. Los Angeles *Times,* March 5, 1985.
19. *Nation,* April 19, 1986, p. 542.
20. Los Angeles *Times,* May 23, 1985.
21. *New York Times*, March 18, 1985.
22. Los Angeles *Times,* July 7, 1985.
23. Washington *Post,* November 12, 1984, national weekly edition.
24. Los Angeles *Times,* February 22, 1984.
25. Los Angeles *Times,* July 7, 1985.
26. *New York Times*, March 17, 1985.
27. Los Angeles *Times,* January 19, 1986.
28. Los Angeles *Times,* February 20, 1986.
29. Los Angeles *Times,* March 9, 1986.
30. *New Yorker*, July 7, 1986, p. 64.
31. *New York Times,* May 20, 1983.
32. Letter to the author, June 27, 1986.
33. Los Angeles *Times,* June 27, 1986.
34. Los Angeles *Times,* July 16, 1986.
35. Los Angeles *Times,* July 24, 1986.
36. *Christian Science Monitor*, June 30, 1986.
37. Los Angeles *Times,* July 20, 1986.
38. *Guardian*, July 9, 1986.
39. *Guardian*, July 23, 1986.

Chapter II. The Dirty Little War

1. *La Prensa* (Managua), May 22, 1985.
2. Los Angeles *Times,* June 12, 1985.
3. *In These Times*, July 12, 1985.
4. Los Angeles *Times,* July 12, 1985.
5. *El Nuevo Diario* (Managua), July 1, 1985.
6. *New York Times*, August 11, 1985.
7. Los Angeles *Times,* March 5, 1985.
8. *Business Week*, March 11, 1985, p. 54.
9. *New York Times*, April 19, 1985.
10. *Time*, March 31, 1986, p. 16.
11. Latin American Studies Association, *The Electoral Process in Nicaragua: Domestic and International Influences* (LASA, 1984), p. i.
12. Roy Gutman, "Nicaragua: America's Diplomatic Charade," *Foreign Policy*, No. 56 (Fall 1984), p. 16.
13. Washington *Post,* October 4, 1984.
14. *New Yorker*, March 31, 1986, p. 20.

15. *Ibid.*, p. 19.

16. Los Angeles *Times,* March 18, 1986.

17. Los Angeles *Times,* April 22, 1985.

18. Los Angeles *Times,* July 20, 1986.

19. *Mesoamerica*, March 1986, p. 1.

20. Conor Cruise O'Brien, "God and Man in Nicaragua," *Atlantic Monthly*, August 1986, p. 64.

21. *New York Times*, March 24, 1986.

22. Los Angeles *Times*, March 18, 1986.

23. *L.A. Weekly*, March 21–27, 1986.

24. Los Angeles *Times,* August 23, 1986.

25. Los Angeles *Times,* January 23, 1986.

26. Los Angeles *Times,* July 13, 1986; Lewis H. Lapham, "Going South," *Harper's,* September 1986, p. 8.

27. Los Angeles *Times*, November 19, 1984.

28. Los Angeles *Times*, April 6, 1986.

29. *Christian Science Monitor*, August 22, 1986.

30. *Newsweek*, November 8, 1982, p. 10.

31. *New York Times*, April 28, 1983.

32. Los Angeles *Times*, July 1, 1986; *Christian Science Monitor*, July 7, 1986.

33. Los Angeles *Times*, March 29, 1986.

34. Jorge Timossi, "Tres entrevistas: Daniel Ortega, Humberto Ortega y Luis Carrión," *Casa de las Américas* (Havana) 117 (November–December 1979): 191.

35. Los Angeles *Times*, March 18, 1985.

36. *In These Times*, April 16–22, 1986.

37. Los Angeles *Times*, March 4, 1985.

38. Los Angeles *Times*, March 5, 1985.

39. Los Angeles *Times*, March 4, 1985.

40. *Wall Street Journal*, March 5, 1985.

41. Los Angeles *Times*, March 4, 1985.

42. Edgar Chamorro, "Confessions of a 'Contra,' " *New Republic*, August 1985, p. 22.

43. *Wall Street Journal*, March 6, 1986.

44. Los Angeles *Times*, March 5, 1985.

45. Los Angeles *Times*, February 11, 1985.

46. Chamorro, "Confessions," p. 23.

47. Los Angeles *Times*, March 5, 1985.

48. *Wall Street Journal*, March 6, 1985.

49. Los Angeles *Times*, March 5, 1985.

50. *Barricada International* (Managua), December 6, 1984.

51. Los Angeles *Times*, March 5, 1985.

52. Chamorro, "Confessions," p. 22.

53. E. Howard Hunt, *Give Us This Day* (New Rochelle, N.Y.: Arlington House, 1973), pp. 61–62.

54. Los Angeles *Times*, April 15, 1986.

55. Los Angeles *Times*, December 20, 1984.

56. *Wall Street Journal*, March 5, 1985.

57. Los Angeles *Times*, November 10, 1984.

58. Los Angeles *Times*, March 5, 1985.

59. *New York Times*, August 8, 1985.

60. *Business Week*, March 11, 1985, p. 54.

61. Los Angeles *Times*, December 24, 1984.

62. *Time*, November 24, 1984.

63. Los Angeles *Times*, December 8, 1985.

64. Los Angeles *Times*, December 13, 1985.

65. Los Angeles *Times*, April 14, 1986.

66. Los Angeles *Times*, August 3, 1985.

67. Los Angeles *Times*, September 9, 1985.

68. *New Yorker*, June 17, 1985, p. 31.

69. Los Angeles *Times*, June 27, 1986.

70. *Congressional Record*, March 26, 1986.

71. Los Angeles *Times*, April 18, 1986.

72. *L.A. Weekly*, May 9–15, 1986.

73. Daniel Ortega, Speech to the National Assembly, Managua, February 21, 1986.

74. Los Angeles *Times*, January 26, 1986.

75. *In These Times*, March 13–19, 1985.

76. *In These Times*, September 25–October 1, 1985.

77. *New York Times*, March 18, 1985.

78. *Christian Science Monitor*, March 19, 1986.

79. *New York Times*, March 24, 1985.

80. Chamorro, "Confessions," p. 23.

81. *Ibid.*, p. 22.

82. Los Angeles *Times*, March 6, 1986.

83. New York *Times*, August 25, 1985.

84. *New Yorker*, July 7, 1986.

85. *New York Times*, August 25, 1985.

86. Des Moines *Register*, March 30, 1986.

87. Los Angeles *Times*, April 15, 1986.

88. *Guardian*, June 11, 1986.

89. *Time*, August 11, 1986, p. 27.

90. Los Angeles *Times*, August 11, 1985.

91. Los Angeles *Times*, January 4, 1986.

92. Los Angeles *Times*, August 11, 1985.

93. *Christian Science Monitor*, April 11, 1986.

94. Los Angeles *Times*, March 20, 1986.

95. *Christian Science Monitor*, April 11, 1986.

96. Los Angeles *Times*, March 8, 1986.

97. *Ibid.*

98. *Wall Street Journal*, April 23, 1985.

99. *Christian Science Monitor*, May 30, 1986; Los Angeles *Times*, May 30, 1986.

100. Los Angeles *Times*, March 22, 1985.

101. Los Angeles *Times*, January 15, 1985.

102. *El Mundo* (Mexico), March 20, 1986; Los Angeles *Times*, March 21, 1986.

103. *El Tiempo* (San Pedro Sula), March 26, 1986.

104. *Links* 3:1–2 (September 1986): p. 7; *Christian Science Monitor*, April 22, 1986.

105. *La Tribuna* (Tegucigalpa), April 11, 1986.

106. *Worldview*, December 1984, p. 17.

107. *Christian Science Monitor*, August 1, 1986.

108. Los Angeles *Times*, June 8, 1986.

109. Los Angeles *Times*, December 21, 1985.

110. San Francisco *Examiner*, March 16, 1986.

111. Los Angeles *Times*, April 18, 1986.

112. Los Angeles *Times*, June 8, 1986.

113. Los Angeles *Times*, March 17, 1986.

114. *Congressional Record*, April 16, 1986.

115. Des Moines *Register*, March 30, 1986.

116. *Ibid.*

117. Cedar Rapids *Gazette*, April 16, 1986.

118. Los Angeles *Times*, May 9, 1986; *Time*, July 7, 1986, p. 26.

119. *Time*, June 23, 1986, p. 36.

120. Los Angeles *Times*, August 14, 1986.

121. Los Angeles *Times*, June 3, 1986.

122. Miami *Herald*, June 1, 1986.

123. Los Angeles *Times*, May 9, 1986.

124. Los Angeles *Times*, April 23, 1986.

125. Los Angeles *Times*, June 12, 1986.

126. *Time*, June 23, 1986, p. 36.

127. *Ibid.*

128. *Time*, July 7, 1986, p. 26.

129. *Nation*, June 7, 1986, p. 783.

130. *Guardian*, June 25, 1986.
131. *Time*, July 7, 1986, p. 26.
132. Los Angeles *Times*, June 25, 1986.
133. Los Angeles *Times*, June 27, 1986.
134. *Time*, June 23, 1986.
135. *Nation*, April 27, 1985, p. 486.
136. Los Angeles *Times*, March 10, 1985.
137. Des Moines *Register*, March 30, 1986.

Chapter III. Global Issues

1. C. G. Jacobsen, "Soviet Attitudes Towards Aid to and Contacts with Central American Revolutionaries" (Report prepared for the Department of State, June 1984), p. 31.
2. *Ibid.*, p. 7.
3. *New York Times*, May 20, 1986.
4. O'Brien, "God and Man in Nicaragua," p. 56.
5. Gordon Connell-Smith, *The Inter-American System* (Oxford: Royal Institute of International Affairs, 1966), pp. 161 and 162.
6. Jeane J. Kirkpatrick, "Dictatorships and Double Standards," *Commentary*, 68:5 (November 1979), pp. 34–35.
7. Los Angeles *Times*, March 10, 1985.

Chapter IV. Nicaragua's Appeal and the World Response

1. Only one biography of Sandino exists in English: Gregorio Selser, *Sandino* (New York: Monthly Review Press, 1981). The Sandino quotations come from this source.
2. Marcus, *Nicaragua*, p. 337.
3. *Ibid.*
4. Latin American members of the Nonaligned Movement and their dates of entry: Cuba (1961), Guyana (1970), Jamaica (1970), Trinidad and Tobago (1970), Argentina (1973), Chile (entered in 1973 but has boycotted the meetings since 1976), Peru (1973), Panama (1976), Nicaragua (1979), Bolivia (1979), Grenada (1979), Surinam (1979), Bahamas (1983), Barbados (1983), Belize (1983), Colombia (1983), Ecuador (1983), St. Lucia (1983). Permanent observers from Latin America are: Antigua, Brazil, Costa Rica, El Salvador, Mexico, Uruguay, and Venezuela. *NACLA Report on the Americas* 29:3 (May–June 1985): p. 16.
5. Los Angeles *Times*, October 23, 1985.
6. Los Angeles *Times*, June 17, 1986.
7. Marcus, *Nicaragua*, pp. 181 and 175.

8. *Ibid.*, p. 113.

9. Los Angeles *Times*, March 12, 1986.

10. *Barricada International* (Managua), August 8, 1985.

11. *Business Week*, September 30, 1985.

12. *New Yorker*, March 31, 1986, p. 20.

13. *Time*, April 1, 1985, p. 1.

14. Los Angeles *Times*, August 25, 1985.

15. *Time* April 8, 1985, p. 47.

16. Los Angeles *Times*, February 3, 1985.

17. Foreign Broadcast Information Service, March 20, 1985, D2.

18. *Christian Science Monitor*, April 4, 1986.

19. Los Angeles *Times*, August 24, 1985.

20. Los Angeles *Times*, February 23, 1985.

21. Los Angeles *Times*, March 10, 1985.

22. *Envio*, 5:55 (January–February 1986), p. 5.

23. *In These Times*, May 22–28, 1985.

24. Los Angeles *Times*, December 16, 1985.

25. *El Mundo* (Mexico), March 20, 1986.

26. *Mesoamerica*, September 1955, p. 1.

27. Los Angeles *Times*, March 21, 1986.

28. *Honduras Update*, 4:9–10 (June–July 1986), p. 10.

29. Canada, Department of External Affairs, "Canada and Nicaragua" (Ottawa, 1986?), p. 2.

30. *Ibid.*

31. Department of External Affairs, "Contadora," (Ottawa, March 1986).

32. *Ibid.*

33. Department of External Affairs, "Canadian Development Assistance to Nicaragua" (Ottawa).

34. Los Angeles *Times*, May 21, 1985.

35. Department of External Affairs, "Canada-Nicaragua Trade" (Ottawa).

36. Los Angeles *Times*, May 6, 1985.

37. *Times of the Americas*, October 10, 1984.

38. *Times of the Americas*, December 4, 1985.

39. *Congressional Record*, May 16, 1985.

40. Los Angeles *Times*, April 6, 1986.

Chapter V. Nicaragua, the United States, and a New World Order

1. *New York Times*, June 14, 1985.

2. Los Angeles *Times*, January 19, 1985.

3. *New York Times*, June 30, 1985.

4. *Barricada International* (Managua), August 22, 1985.
5. *El Dia* (Mexico), November 17, 1983.
6. Los Angeles *Times*, March 16, 1986.
7. *Mother Jones*, January 1986, p. 24.
8. Los Angeles *Times*, March 17, 1985.
9. *Christian Science Monitor*, May 2, 1983.
10. Los Angeles *Times*, August 15, 1986.
11. Los Angeles *Times*, March 17, 1985.
12. *New York Times*, June 30, 1985.
13. J. Lloyd Mecham, *A Survey of United States–Latin American Relations* (Boston: Houghton Mifflin, 1965), p. 165.
14. *Christian Science Monitor*, April 4, 1986.
15. *In These Times*, September 25–October 1, 1985.
16. *Time*, December 10, 1984.
17. Los Angeles *Times*, June 28, 1986.
18. *Ibid.*; *Christian Science Monitor*, June 30, 1986.
19. *Christian Science Monitor*, July 15, 1986.
20. Los Angeles *Times*, June 29, 1986.
21. Los Angeles *Times*, August 3, 1986.
22. Los Angeles *Times*, July 11, 1986.
23. *Christian Science Monitor*, April 4, 1986.
24. *Ibid.*

Chapter VI. Issues and Dilemmas

1. Biderman, "The Development of Capitalism in Nicaragua," p. 12.
2. Carleton Beals, *Banana Gold* (Philadelphia: Lippincott, 1932), pp. 300–301.
3. *Ibid.*, pp. 294–296.
4. Washington *Post*, September 2, 1985, national weekly edition.
5. *Time*, March 31, 1986, p. 15.
6. Richard Falk, "Thinking about Terrorism," *Nation*, June 28, 1986, p. 873.
7. Christopher Hitchens, "Wanton Acts of Usage—Terrorism: A Cliche in Search of a Meaning," *Harper's*, September 1986, p. 70.
8. Washington *Post*, November 12, 1984, national weekly edition.
9. Los Angeles *Times*, January 21, 1985.
10. *Christian Science Monitor*, August 1, 1986.
11. Los Angeles *Times*, October 23, 1985.
12. *Nation*, September 7, 1985, pp. 186–87.
13. *Time*, August 25, 1986, p. 23.
14. *In These Times*, July 9–22, 1986.

15. *Ibid.*

16. *Nation*, May 3, 1986, p. 605.

17. Los Angeles *Herald-Examiner*, July 27, 1986.

18. *In These Times*, September 25–October 1, 1985.

19. Joshua Cohen and Joel Rogers, *Inequity and Intervention: The Federal Budget and Central America* (Boston: South End Press, 1986); Cohen and Rogers, "The True Cost of Intervention," *Nation*, April 12, 1986.

Chapter VII. Charting the Future

1. Secretary of State George Shultz to European Economic Community foreign ministers, September 7, 1984.

2. *Time*, December 10, 1984.

3. Washington *Post*, November 26, 1984, national weekly edition.

4. Internal National Security Council Memorandum, October 30, 1984; Washington *Post*, November 6, 1984.

5. *Congressional Record*, March 26, 1986.

6. *Central American Report* (Berkeley), April 11, 1986.

7. Los Angeles *Times*, August 8, 1986.

8. *In These Times*, July 10–23, 1985.

9. Los Angeles *Times*, October 6, 1985.

10. George P. Shultz, "New Realities and New Ways of Thinking," *Foreign Affairs* 63:4 (Spring 1985): 707.

11. *New York Times*, March 20, 1984.

12. Joshua Maravchik, *Nicaragua's Slow March to Communism* (Washington, D.C.: The Cuban American National Foundation, 1986).

13. Howard J. Wiarda, "United States Policy in Central America: Toward a New Relationship" (Statement prepared for the National Bipartisan Commission on Central America, U.S. Department of State, 1983).

14. *Time*, March 31, 1986, p. 20.

15. Washington *Post*, March 11, 1985, national weekly edition.

16. *Time*, March 31, 1986, p. 17.

17. *Time*, August 11, 1986, p. 27.

18. Los Angeles *Times*, July 30, 1986.

INDEX

Calero, Mario, 75, 76
California, 13, 143
Callejas, Alfonso Robelo, 65
Cambodia, 47, 130
Canada, 32, 37, 103, 118
  policy toward Central America,
    112–115
Canal, transisthmian, 14, 16, 17
Capitalism, 11, 69, 98
Cardenal, Ernesto, 117
Carrión, Luis, 51–52
Carter, Jimmy, 19, 20, 21, 22, 23, 52
Carter, Michael, 7
Casey, William, 53, 56, 150, 159
Castro, Fidel, 10, 18, 44
Cayman Islands, 79
Central America, 3, 14, 18, 24, 28, 42,
    43, 46, 47, 48, 50, 59, 61, 63,
    73–74, 80, 98, 103, 104, 105,
    107, 116, 131–132, 139, 151, 154,
    161, 164, 171, 173, 175
  economic realities of, 108
  and intervention, 143–149
  as microcosm of Third World,
    143–149
  and Reagan Doctrine, 129–131
  U.S. policy toward, 182, 183
Central American Common Market,
    109, 189
Central Intelligence Agency (CIA), 2,
    10, 26, 27, 43, 44, 46, 84, 142,
    159
  and contra leadership, 64–79, 160
  manual on psychological warfare, 58,
    151–152
  mining of Nicaraguan ports, 54–56,
    135, 151
  and overthrow of Allende, 81
  and overthrow of Arbenz, 81, 84,
    125–126, 157
  and Reagan Doctrine, 130, 142
  and terrorism, 149, 150, 151
  and war in Nicaragua, 48–63, 135,
    156, 160
Central Treaty Organization
    (CENTO), 122, 132
Cerezo, Venicio, 39, 109–110, 170,
    171, 177
Chamorro, Edgar, 23, 52, 53, 54, 62,
    64, 70, 160
Change, dynamic of, 8–9, 176, 184
  challenge of, 142

Change (cont.)
  and institutional structures, 88–89,
    141, 191
  U.S. response to, 9–12, 130, 142,
    188
Chile, 9, 39, 41, 48, 70, 81, 83, 158,
    169
China, People's Republic of, 34, 118,
    122, 141
Christian Base Communities, 87, 88
Christianity, 8
Christian Science Monitor, 138
Civiletti, Benjamin, 135
Clark, Joe, 113, 114
Clark, Ramsey, 155
Clarridge, Duane, 54
Client state, concept of, 91–93, 176,
    181
Coffee, 3, 33, 73
Cohen, William, 78
Colombia, 38, 40, 83, 105, 106, 165,
    170
Colonialism, xii
Communism, 11, 12, 17, 21, 22, 27,
    28, 34, 36, 40, 69, 70, 80, 82, 84,
    85, 89, 98, 145, 160, 189
Conahan, Frank C., 76
Contadora Peace Process, 24, 26, 39,
    99, 127, 131, 137, 138, 163–175,
    186, 187, 192
  as Bolivarian idea, 177, 178
  Canadian support of, 113–114
  Latin American support of, 104,
    105–106, 176, 179–180
  U.N. support of, 118
Contadora Peace Treaty, 25, 106,
    187
Contadora Support Group, 105,
    169–170, 175
Contras, xi, 1, 16, 24, 26, 46, 133, 160
  and corruption, 78–79
  and Costa Rica, 72, 110–111
  and El Salvador, 72
  financial irregularities of, 75–78
  and Honduras, 72–75
  "humanitarian" aid to, 59–60
  lack of program, 70–71
  Latin American opposition to,
    104–105
  leadership of, 63–79
  as obstacle to peace, 173
  and terrorism, 71–79, 150, 152